D0699888

VELOCITY

FROM THE FRONT LINE TO THE BOTTOM LINE

Dale Pollak

New Year Publishing LLC
Danville, California

VELOCITY

FROM THE FRONT LINE TO THE BOTTOM LINE

by Dale Pollak

Published by:
New Year Publishing LLC
144 Diablo Ranch Ct.
Danville, CA 94506 USA

orders@newyearpublishing.com
http://www.newyearpublishing.com

ISBN: 978-0-9760095-7-3

CONTENTS

⑧ Injecting Honesty and Investment Smarts into Wholesale Dispositions 101

⑨ Viewing Reconditioning as an Investment, not as an Expense 119

ACKNOWLEDGEMENTS

There are many people that I must thank and acknowledge for their contributions to this book.

Writing this book would not have been possible without the assistance and guidance of Lance Helgeson, who served as my "eyes" as well as my sounding board throughout the writing process.

I would like to thank my children Austin, Alex and Samson, and my mother, Beth, for their love and support. Special thanks must be reserved for my father and mentor, Len Pollak, not only for his love and support, but for the insights he has shared with me over the years regarding the used car business.

I have been extremely privileged to have worked closely with several people, all of whom have not been directly referenced in this book, although their names certainly appear between the lines. Specifically, I would like to thank Tommy Gibbs, John Honiotes,

Bill Krouse, and Mark Rikess for their help and generosity from the very first stages of vAuto through growing it into the company it is today.

It is with the utmost respect and appreciation I thank Keith Jezek, Mike Chiovari and David Hawkins for being my friends, partners and role models in more ways than I can possibly list.

I must also thank the thousands of dealers and sales managers who have shared their experiences with me.

Finally, I would like to thank my loving wife Nancy, with whom all my dreams are possible.

Dale Pollak, December 2007

FOREWORD: A BOOK THAT ISN'T FOR EVERYONE

The car business has been very good to me. My father was a Buick dealer in Gary, Indiana, and, like many dealers' sons, I followed in his footsteps. I worked in the family business until the time came when I wanted my own store.

My opportunity arrived in 1985. I took the reins of a Cadillac dealership in Elmhurst, Illinois. I ran the store for 12 years and, it's safe to say, I probably acquired a different approach to managing my store than most dealers.

The difference comes from the fact that I'm legally blind. I couldn't actually see the spiffy showroom we had or the shiny vehicles that we sold. I had to entrust others with making sure our store was spit-polished and welcoming.

But, despite my lack of eyesight, I could still manage dealership operations by following the numbers. They say necessity breeds invention and that's exactly the attitude I took to overcome what would otherwise be a serious liability.

Thankfully, I have always had a knack for numbers so it wasn't long before I became an astute student of our dealership's financial statements. I knew, almost to the penny, how well each of my dealership's departments performed on any given day.

One department at my dealership got an undue amount of attention when compared with how other dealers managed their stores. While many of my colleagues kept their focus on their new vehicle sales departments, I put my focus on used vehicles.

Why? In part, this emphasis came from a lesson my father had passed along. He, too, was a student of the financials and he recognized that in used vehicles, it was our money that was on the line. Whenever we talked about used vehicles—whether the topic was pricing, reconditioning or desking—he'd invariably say four words that I can still hear today: "It's the money, honey."

My father also believed that the used vehicle department is the heart and soul of a dealership's variable operations. If you are not doing well in used vehicles, there's an inevitable spill-over effect in your new vehicle department. It is not always easy to spot the symptoms, but there is no mistaking when a troubled used vehicle department creates problems for desking deals and appraising trade-ins—provided you are paying attention.

So, unlike other dealers who really only worried about volume, age and gross in used vehicles, I drilled into our used vehicle financials more deeply, applying an investment-focused mentality to our department operations. On any given day, I wanted to know whether we stood a chance of making money on a vehicle or not, and I wanted to know what we were doing to either make money or avoid a loss.

At the time, I knew that how I managed our department was different than most dealers, but it never occurred to me that I was any kind of a maverick or anomaly. I was just doing what my dad had told me to do; it really was about the money and being smart about my cash investment.

While I was a dealer, there was one thing that frustrated me to no end. I needed department financials and data to be effective. Yet, it was like pulling teeth to extract the information I wanted from our dealer management system (DMS) for individual departments, in part because the data simply wasn't available. Our DMS couldn't effectively talk to the systems we used in service, finance and insurance (F&I) and parts.

Around 1997, I got a call from a salesperson at Digital Motorworks, Inc. DMi was trying to sell kiosks because they believed their kiosks would give customers a chance to view inventory and configure vehicles on their own, revolutionizing how people bought cars.

I was intrigued. The kiosk idea was kind of cool, but I was more interested in knowing how the system's back end worked. How, exactly, could this system access and accurately extract my vehicle inventory information from my DMS and then display it?

This little insight, borne of the frustration I had endured for years because I couldn't easily access the information I wanted to run my store, became my entry point into the land of software development for dealerships.

I started talking to DMi executives more frequently about my ideas and, in time, I sold my dealership to run the company. I had a hunch: if we could use

Digital Motorworks' technology as an interface, we'd be on to something big. With my help, the company's renewed vision was simple and even more far-reaching than the original retail kiosk concept. We wanted to be the go-to company for any software vendor that needed to interface its product and data with a DMS.

DMi operates largely behind the scenes. I fondly remember the comment one of my colleagues once made: "It's pretty amazing that any software provider who wants to work with dealerships has to at least come and visit us to ensure their product will work."

I was very lucky at DMi. I had the opportunity to meet and befriend some of the top leaders in our industry. Our company developed an industry-changing product that, even today, powers many of the linkages that enable dealer software solutions to speak to DMSs.

Our success came to a head in 2002, when our track record spurred Automatic Data Processing, Inc. to approach us about an acquisition. My partners and I cut the deal with ADP and made handsome profits for the time, energy and sweat equity we had put into the company.

I share all this personal background because the dual experiences of running a dealership and an industry-leading software company give me a unique perspective. I've been in the trenches, sitting at a metal desk in Elmhurst, making deals. My years at DMi put me in conference rooms with top factory, public dealer group and private dealer group leaders. Put another way, you could say that my experience enables me to envision the trees and the forest at the same time.

While I was busy with DMi, the issues in the used car department in Elmhurst continued to play in my mind. While I traveled the country, I kept asking anyone who'd take my questions about their used vehicle departments and how they managed them. I even started knocking around other ideas about how a dealer might use internal data about used vehicles—what sold, when it sold, what didn't sell, etc.—to better manage used vehicle operations.

Looking back, I can now see what I was doing. All of my intellectual noodling about used vehicles was sowing the seeds for my next entrepreneurial opportunity: giving our industry a better way of managing their used vehicle departments.

With exactly that thought in mind, I started vAuto. I have to again give credit to my father for his simple saying, "It's the money, honey."

In the early days at vAuto, it became clear that getting the data necessary to create a used vehicle inventory optimization system was next to impossible. In fact, it still is nearly impossible. There are way too many variables in play on any given vehicle—make, model, trim levels, options, etc., not to mention ever-changing market conditions—that make the idea of a know-it-all, magic black box type of system something of a fallacy.

But guess what? If you do what my father suggests and follow the money on every vehicle, you suddenly have a way of beating the problem of inconsistent and wide-ranging data about individual vehicles. In some ways, if you follow the money and track each unit as an investment, those individual variables, while still important, take a back seat to the central question of knowing, at any given moment, whether you stand to make or lose money on a vehicle.

The pages of this book, *Velocity: From the Front Line to the Bottom Line*, represent the distillation of best practices, ideas and observations that I've gleaned from years of studying the financials of used vehicle departments and trying to come up with a better way of managing what I believe can be the most exciting and profit-generating department in any dealership. Just like my father, I believe the used vehicle department is the heart and soul of a dealership—its success feeds the sales and profits in new vehicle sales, F&I, and parts and service. No other department in a dealership has this kind of pass-along power.

As I write this book, the used vehicle marketplace is more challenging than it ever has been. More dealers are struggling to build volumes and gross profits, and they are scratching their heads as to why it's so difficult.

That is one reason I chose to write this book. With all the thinking I have done about used vehicles, I have begun to understand why this business has become so difficult. There are a multitude of reasons, but many of them flow directly from the advent of the Internet.

Thanks to the Internet, the used vehicle business has become more like a commodities market. Buyers have a multitude of choices and prices are easy to find. To them, vehicles aren't as unique as they used to be, no matter how much we, as dealers, believe and tell our customers that "you won't find another one like this anywhere." For dealers, this commodities-like market means that waiting for the right buyer to come around on a unit just doesn't work anymore, especially if your pricing is out of line.

To put it another way, today's used vehicle marketplace is less giving and less forgiving than

its ever been before. That's why I firmly believe the
"it's the money, honey" mentality, backed by astute,
investment-minded management processes, is essential
for today's dealers to survive and thrive.

This book details those success stories and helps
dealers and used vehicle managers understand how to
deploy this investment-minded approach to managing
used vehicle operations.

Let me offer this disclaimer: this book isn't for
everyone. In fact, if you are satisfied with the returns
and profits in your used vehicle department, you
should stop reading right here. Why bother with
reading further about how an investment-minded
mentality and investment-based management
processes can potentially help your used vehicle
department if you really don't think you have
anything to gain?

If you're still with me, and you've got the stomach
to take what may feel like some tough medicine,
then read on. By the time you finish this book, you
should have enough insights and ideas to begin what
I guarantee will be a powerful and transformative
approach to managing your used vehicle business.

You should also know that it will take guts and
gumption to apply the principles and processes that

I describe. You'll need to reverse the bad habits and bad decisions that occur in used vehicle departments every day. But, as long as you've got the will to learn some new tricks and have a genuine interest in doing a better job in used vehicles, this book and the investment-based management processes I discuss are likely to be just right for you.

Enjoy the read … and enjoy the additional money you'll be making at the expense of your competitors who will probably never understand what hit them.

① A Case for Investment-Minded Used Vehicle Management

It's a cloudy, chilly October afternoon at Shirey Cadillac, a dealership that has served the Southwest Chicago suburb of Oak Lawn for more than three decades.

The showroom lacks the hustle-bustle that most dealers would immediately recognize as a place where business is going well. In fact, on this Wednesday afternoon, there isn't a single customer in the showroom or even on the lot—a dearth that owes partially to the unfriendly fall weather, the slowdown in demand for many domestic dealers and the reality that the community around the store has become less likely to fit the mold of a traditional Cadillac buyer.

But as dealer Tom Shirey takes a seat in a wood-paneled conference room to discuss his business with me, the store's new vehicle volumes are a testament to the gold mine that he's discovered in his used vehicle department.

"We're 20 percent ahead of our volumes from where we were last year, and gross profit is up 25 percent to 30 percent," says Shirey, who acknowledges that this infusion of profits has given his entire store a new lease on life. Without it, he might well have had to close up shop for good.

"I've been thinking about the used vehicle business for a long time," Shirey says. "We'd sit around the table and talk about how we've been cannibalizing our used vehicle department to sell new vehicles. I think we've found a better way."

Shirey's epiphany resulted in a top-to-bottom change in how he runs his used vehicle department. It's driven by what he terms "bottom feeding"—an effort to scour the marketplace for the lowest cost units that will enable him to price them more competitively at retail than any other dealer. It also includes what the store's controller says is "like a religion."

On a near-daily basis, Shirey and his managers calculate the equity position of each vehicle in the store's inventory, examining how the vehicle's retail price tag compares with similar vehicles on the market. They account for holding costs and depreciation and make adjustments to the gross profit they believe the vehicle can generate. And, at the moment they sense a vehicle is in trouble or it cannot generate the profits the store expects, they will make plans to dispose of it through retail or wholesale channels.

"There comes a point when you have to be a man about taking a loss," says Shirey. "I'll take a loss on a fresh car if it doesn't make sense from an investment perspective."

The approach that Shirey and his managers apply to their used vehicle business is far more scientific than the vast majority of dealers who entrust used vehicle managers to manage the investment of what is typically the single-largest asset on a dealer's balance sheet. Shirey acknowledges that his new approach is a far cry from the way he and his managers had long run the department. Like many dealers, Shirey didn't track depreciation or holding costs; used vehicle pricing followed a "mark-it-up-from-cost" habit that didn't account for the vehicle's true retail market value, and wholesale losses weren't accurately accounted for; some vehicles got dumped to cover up wholesale losses on other vehicles that should have, but didn't, get sold.

"This is more than just managing the age of vehicles. If you do that, you're coming at it from a point of weakness. You have no opportunities," Shirey says.

Today, Shirey's store turns its inventory of about 80 vehicles 15 times a year. With the quick turn, market-based pricing and disciplined, investment-minded approach, Shirey says his store "can outsell the competition every time" and generate gross profits that, while they aren't the home runs he once sought, are sufficient to improve the bottom line for his store.

And, just to be clear, the competition Shirey refers to isn't limited to other dealers in the Chicago region. More than half of the vehicles he sells go to out-of-state buyers who are seeking the best price. Customers find his inventory selections through their own Internet searches.

To anyone schooled in the traditional management practices that dealers and used vehicle managers have followed for decades, Shirey's approach is nothing short of ground-breaking. To reiterate: he'll dump a fresh car if some analysis of what he paid to get the vehicle and what it would take to price and sell it quickly, reveals the vehicle's a likely dog. Most used vehicle managers and dealers do not figure that out until 30, 45 or 60 days have passed and they're staring at a wholesale loss.

Further, Shirey's pricing strategies are as scientific as you can get. He recognizes that today's used vehicle shoppers won't give him a second look if his vehicles are not priced competitively. He knows that simply marking up a vehicle from his cost to set a retail asking price has little, if any, relevance to what the retail market value of the vehicle should be.

I share Shirey's story because he's someone who understands the reality of today's used vehicle marketplace. It isn't The Wild Wild West it once was. You can't just acquire a vehicle, put a retail asking price on it and hope a buyer will come in to pay the price you want to get. That's what I call the $4,000 Fantasy.

Today's business is far more complex and competitive than it has ever been. Shirey's made significant adjustments to how he runs his used vehicle department. He's brought an investment-minded focus to every aspect of his used vehicle operations, and he's enjoying the successes his decisions have brought: faster turns of his inventory, fewer wholesale losses, and better overall profitability and, perhaps most importantly, a sense of confidence that he's on to something that few dealers have even considered.

"The industry's never going to change until dealers take a firm belief in the fact that it is their money on the line in their used vehicle departments and they are responsible for the investment return. When dealers do that, they'll quit delegating the authority and oversight for the investment to paid hands," Shirey says.

WHY WRITE THIS BOOK?

Shirey is living proof that there's a better way of managing used vehicle departments and it all hinges around the simple and profound notion that we need to treat every vehicle like an investment.

Risk. Return. Equity. These are some of the fundamental principles that underlie every investment. Through this book, I hope to give you a better understanding of how you can apply these principles to every aspect of your used vehicle operations—from acquiring, reconditioning, pricing and desking to disposing of used vehicles.

As you then apply these principles, you'll start to realize the benefits of greater sales volumes, faster inventory turns, improved profitability and fewer losses that have turned the used vehicle departments at dealerships like Shirey's into a can't-miss, profit-generating powerhouse.

THE SEEDS OF A BACK SEAT BUSINESS

Tom Shirey isn't the only dealer who's taking an investment-minded approach to managing his used vehicle business.

Jerrod Musser, a former stockbroker-turned-GM who manages the used vehicle operation for Summit Ford in Silverthorne, Colorado, sees little difference between his previous job and his current position in the dealership.

"You have to treat your investment, or used vehicle inventory, like a trading portfolio where a decision to hold a stock is based upon the type of stock and your ability to sell it, and a decision to sell is based on how much it costs you to keep the stock rather than how much you'd lose if you sold it," he says.

"Nobody looks at the business that way," Musser continues. "I've talked to more dealers than I can count who don't understand what I'm saying."

"You have to treat your investment, or used vehicle inventory, like a trading portfolio where a decision to hold a stock is based upon the type of stock and your ability to sell it, and a decision to sell is based on how much it costs you to keep the stock rather than how much you'd lose if you sold it," says Jarrod Musser.

Both Shirey and Musser are on to something profound. The two don't know each other, but they share a similar outlook: today's used vehicle marketplace is different than it used to be and it requires a different approach to be successful. Not surprisingly, they both came to the same conclusion—that an investment-minded strategy is the solution—after consistently finding it difficult to build used vehicle volumes and sustain gross profits using the management principles that have guided dealers and used vehicle managers for nearly 100 years.

I've studied both the historical and current dynamics in the used vehicle business, and I would have to agree that Shirey and Musser are correct: today's business is very different than the way it used to be. It's more volatile, pricing is more transparent, brand loyalty is more elusive, wholesale losses are more frequent, vehicles that should move just aren't selling … and the list goes on.

For most dealers and used vehicle managers, the changes have spurred some head-scratching, hand-wringing and, in some cases, a crackdown in their used vehicle departments to make improvements. The problem: while many of these dealers adopt turn policies, bucket pricing, inventory optimization and other approaches, they have not made any changes to the fundamentals of the business that, given today's market, require the kind of changed thinking and re-examination that Shirey and Musser have used to turn troubled used vehicle departments into money-makers.

THE GOOD 'OLE DAYS

Before we get to how you can change your thinking and management approaches, it's necessary to examine why today's used vehicle marketplace is different and why traditional management principles and practices are no longer cutting it.

It goes back to the earliest days of the used vehicle business.

In 1929, the vice president of Studebaker Corp., Paul Hoffman, and the company's manager of cooperative development, James H. Greene, wrote a book called *Marketing Used Cars* that was intended to give franchised dealers a roadmap for increasing their interest in and sales of used vehicles. The writer's note that dealers have regarded used cars as an evil and have attempted to delegate the disposal of such cars to other agencies. They go on to say that the used car department is a stepchild of the automobile business.[1]

This underscores a mentality that, to some extent, remains an undercurrent among today's franchised dealers. Franchised dealers have always preferred selling new vehicles rather than used vehicles.

When I was a dealer operating a Cadillac store near Chicago, I had the same attitude. I went to work every day with an eye on selling our new units. Our sales meetings sometimes addressed used vehicles, but it was a secondary priority, often driven by instances

---

1   Paul Hoffman and James. H. Greene, *Marketing Used Cars* (Harper & Brothers Publishers), Page 5.

when we needed to step up on trade-ins to help drive new vehicle volumes.

There are several inherent factors that have contributed to dealers, including me, relegating used vehicle departments to back seat status:

- **Manufacturers train dealers to focus on new vehicles.** Most dealers can recite the key fundamentals from their financial statements on a dime. They'll know how many new units they've sold, their average gross profits, the status of their accounts receivables and the amounts they spend on key expenses. It's not surprising that they carry these figures inside their heads, all are readily available on factory financial statements.

  Here's what's largely been missing for years: the factory financial statements barely account for used vehicles. For most dealers, the used vehicle inventory is their single-largest asset, outside of property and facilities. Yet there's very little detail about this asset on factory financial statements. In fact, most factory statements include more details about a store's accounts receivables than they do about a dealer's entire used vehicle inventory, even though the average dealer's used vehicle investment is likely 15 to 25 times bigger than all receivables combined.

It's no wonder that dealers and used vehicle managers are more ad hoc about how they manage their used vehicle operations compared to other departments. The underlying financial statements simply don't engender a more detailed and data-driven approach.

For most dealers, the used vehicle inventory is their single-largest asset, outside of property and facilities. Yet there's very little detail about this asset on factory financial statements. In fact, most factory statements include more details about a store's accounts receivables than they do about a dealer's entire used vehicle inventory, even though the average dealer's used vehicle investment is likely 15 to 25 times bigger than all receivables combined.

"That's true," says auto dealer and CPA Jeff Forsberg of Peterson & Sullivan, located in Seattle. "The information about used vehicles is sparse, but it has been getting better, particularly among the import manufacturers."

• **Solid margins on new vehicles.** Believe it or not, there was a time when dealers could make excellent returns on new vehicle sales. Deals with $2,000 and $3,000 gross profits were commonplace. But that's no longer the case. For domestic dealers, factory over-production and increased competition has thinned new vehicle margins. Meanwhile, the high-flying import dealers often have to effectively give away new vehicles to satisfy intense factory requirements to turn inventory and earn additional allocations. It's no surprise, then, that many dealers are taking a deeper look at their used vehicle operations to improve profitability.

- **A forgiving business.** I've asked myself some tough questions about the way used vehicle departments are run. Why did dealers simply not worry about the wholesale losses or acquisition mistakes that were made? The best answer I can come to is that no one had to. The used vehicle business, historically, has been a forgiving business.

  I distinctly remember the days when it really didn't matter how much money we put into a vehicle. We intuitively knew that someday, someone would walk into our store and buy the vehicle that we'd paid too much for, at a profit.

  This dynamic held true for years because, by and large, the vehicles we sold were unique. If we had a used Cadillac for sale, chances are it was unlike any other used Cadillac available in town. Given that reality, and the pricing differences between new and used vehicles, we all enjoyed a market where hitting a so-called home run wasn't just easy, it was almost routine.

- **Dealers controlled used vehicle transactions.** I recently read a quote in a trade magazine from mega-dealer Ken Garff of Garff Automotive in Salt Lake City. He was recalling how his stores used to be full of Saturday shoppers kicking the tires on vehicles, both new and used. "I don't see that anymore," Garff says.

His observation points to another dynamic in yesterday's used vehicle marketplace. We, as dealers, had control of the transaction. Customers came to us holding newspaper clippings of the vehicles we had to sell or they'd visit our store after seeing a unit on our front line that got their attention.

Once they were at our dealerships, all we had to do was help them land on a vehicle that fit their needs. When it came to price, we had the upper hand: customers could either pay what we were asking, or they could drive away and keep shopping. We can all recall instances when customers, who weren't 100 percent happy with our price, opted to buy our vehicle simply because it put an end to the time and trouble they'd already invested in shopping. For them, it was better to get it done rather than walk away and keep looking.

Each of these factors contributes to the traditional back seat status of used vehicle departments at many franchised dealerships. The good news is that a growing number of dealers and used vehicle managers are beginning to recognize the opportunities they've been missing in used vehicles, and they're putting a greater focus on improving sales volumes and profits.

The problem, however, is that when they apply traditional management approaches to the task, they don't see the results they expect. The reason: even with a renewed focus on used vehicles, many dealers and used vehicle managers have yet to fully understand and embrace the profound change that's made today's used vehicle marketplace far less forgiving and far more challenging than it has ever been.

THE PERFECT STORM

Sometime around 2005, Ken Gilman, the former CEO of public dealer group Asbury Automotive, told Wall Street analysts that the company would be putting greater emphasis on used vehicles to drive additional profits and offset margin declines in the company's new vehicle departments.

Gilman's comment got some press but it wasn't the wake-up call for the industry that it might have been. Like many other astute operators, Gilman saw the writing on the wall: for his business to sustain its ROI targets, used vehicle operations needed to move from back-seat status to front-burner priority.

Today, that's pretty much the reality for every dealer, even those who have enjoyed great success and growth in recent years on the back of a strong franchise mix. Dealer Joel Weinberger of Continental Motors, a suburban Chicago group that carries all of the top-volume import makes across seven stores, says used vehicles have been an Achilles heel for his family's business.

"When you're extremely profitable on new vehicles, it hides the sins of your used vehicle department," Weinberger says. "Now that the new vehicle business is less profitable, we need to turn around our used vehicle operations to help."

But the problem for Weinberger and other dealers, who have pledged to do a better job in used vehicles, is that the business has fundamentally changed. There's a Perfect Storm brewing that has made some of the old management principles—worrying about age, gross profits and volume—insufficient barometers to guide sales volume and profit growth in today's used vehicle departments.

WHAT CAUSED THE PERFECT STORM?

Factor 1: Increased factory influence on used vehicles

Few dealers would dispute that new vehicle overproduction and incentives have made the used vehicle business more challenging than it ever has been. Most of you can remember when these two forces combined to wreak havoc on used vehicle values, not long after the Sept. 11, 2001 attacks.

Let's address new vehicle overproduction first. This is the single biggest reason why today's used vehicles are no longer as unique in the eyes of customers as they once were.

To understand, we need to turn back the clock.

Some of you no doubt remember the advent of program cars and guaranteed buy-back programs that became popular in the mid-1980s. Factories ran those programs because it provided a way for them to maintain production and sell the vehicles through their own channels.

At the time, I was a Cadillac dealer and I remember that we could buy a truckload of factory program Sedan DeVilles and sell them all for high gross profits. To us, these were easy money cars.

I also recall, however, when those easy money cars became more challenging. Other dealers saw our success and started buying program cars, too.

Pretty soon, we were all at the same auctions, buying the same types of vehicles and putting them on our lots.

What did that do to customers? Instead of coming to my store for a unique used vehicle, a customer could find similar inventory at my competitor's store. The similarity of vehicles gave way to price competition. We simply couldn't mark the vehicles up the way we'd done before. We also started to notice that vehicles on which we'd consistently hit home runs were stacking up and aging past 120 days in our inventories.

Since those days, factory lease and program vehicles have only grown in scope. In more recent years, factories have launched and promoted certified used vehicle programs. These effectively reduce risk for consumers interested in purchasing used units and equalize purchasing decisions.

Taken together, the impact of these factory programs creates a significant ripple effect on the used vehicle market: your inventory is a lot less unique than you may think it is, and your pricing strategies had better reflect the competition and adjust for the sometimes unexpected increases of supply that occur when factories or rental companies flood the market with used units. If you're inattentive to these dynamics, it's almost a guarantee that you'll wind up with an over-aged inventory.

In addition to factory overproduction, the factories' efforts to pump up demand for new vehicles, through sometimes insane amounts of incentive money, has had a potentially disastrous impact on used vehicle departments.

That's a chief reason why the so-called sweet spot for today's used vehicle marketplace is a four- or five-year-old vehicle with low miles and in good condition. Most dealers and used vehicle managers understand that factory incentive and financing programs make

The impact of these factory programs creates a significant ripple effect on the used vehicle market: your inventory is a lot less unique than you may think it is, and your pricing strategies had better reflect the competition and adjust for the sometimes unexpected increases of supply that occur when factories or rental companies flood the market with used units. If you're inattentive to these dynamics, it's almost a guarantee that you'll wind up with an over-age inventory.

it extremely difficult to sell a customer a one- or two-year-old vehicle when they can essentially buy a new vehicle for the same money.

"If I can find four- or five-year-old Maximas for $3,500, I'll buy them by the truckload," says dealer Gary Duncan of the Roanoke, Virginia-based, Duncan Automotive Network.

Duncan's comment underscores the reality that most dealers really sell two types of used vehicles, those that are near-new, and those that aren't.

It didn't used to be that way. Years ago, you couldn't find a used vehicle on a dealer's lot that would catch a customer's eye and compete with a new vehicle. The average trade cycle ran five years or more. Today, the trade cycle runs closer to three years, thanks in part to leasing and new vehicle incentives that encourage customers to buy new.

The dual nature of today's used vehicle inventories ultimately puts greater pressure on managers to buy vehicles right, and to price them properly. Used vehicle managers and dealers tell me they've seen factory incentives chop $2,000 or more off some used vehicles in a single day.

That's one reason Musser has essentially scrapped his use of a 60-day turn policy. In the past, the 60-day mark was a guidepost to wholesale a vehicle. In today's market, Musser believes that daily measurement of his potential return on investment, done by tracking his acquisition costs, retail pricing, age and expected gross profit return, is the only way to determine whether he'll call a wholesale buyer or drop his retail asking price to get rid of a unit.

"I know my break even point on each vehicle and if it gets there in 5 days, 10 days or 20 days, I'll get rid of it," he says.

Most dealers don't deploy the science-like approach that Musser applies to his inventory—which means the risks of wholesale losses increase, especially on the near-new units, as factory incentive programs change. As Musser notes, used vehicles are assets that depreciate every day and therefore require near-daily diligence to manage the health of the investment return he can expect to get.

I'm not saying that near-new units shouldn't have a place in a dealer's used inventory. After all, you need a wide mix and variety of used vehicles to appeal to all buyers. And, in many cases, you should take in near-new vehicles on trade-ins to support your new vehicle sales department.

But this segment of used vehicle inventory is particularly volatile in today's market and, as Musser points out, even a strict 60-day turn policy may not be enough to ward off wholesale losses.

New vehicle over-production has created another problem in used vehicle departments: there are simply too many makes, models and vehicle configurations for any used vehicle manager to possibly keep track of.

Factor 2: The proliferation of makes and models

New vehicle over-production has created another problem in used vehicle departments: there are simply too many makes, models and vehicle configurations for any used vehicle manager to possibly track.

These days, customers want personalized vehicles and accordingly, factories have responded in spades. When Ford, for example, re-launched its F-150, the factory touted the thousands of different option and trim configurations.

During my time as a dealer, my used vehicle manager pretty much knew what any Cadillac was worth. In fact, it wasn't that difficult. We probably had six to eight different models in a given year, with roughly an equal number of trim/option packages. For the most part, my used vehicle manager could keep all those figures in his head, and offer a pretty accurate read on what a vehicle was worth.

But it's not that way today. Factories are pumping out a wider array of vehicles to appeal to buyers at a greater number of price points and model segments. At the 2006 North American International Auto Show in Detroit, manufacturers showcased more than 60 new models headed for dealer showrooms. NAIAS publications note the show has averaged about three-dozen new model introductions since 1999.

In an age when dealers and used vehicle managers must sell both in-brand and off-brand vehicles to be competitive, is it possible for any one person to truly know how much a given vehicle is worth? Could that individual know the precise effect that a GPS system, a specific paint color or a different accessory or option has on a vehicle's value and potential to sell?

We can all agree that the answer to both questions is no. In fact, it's my belief that the proliferation of software tools to help used vehicle managers optimize their inventories is a direct result of the recognition that no single person can possibly keep up with the sheer volume of information that today's used vehicle marketplace requires managers to track. Faced with this reality, software tools do offer a far better way to do the job in today's used vehicle marketplace.

I couldn't agree more—and not just because my company, vAuto, sells a software solution.

Any dealer and used vehicle manager who uses technology to assist in managing their inventory is a step ahead of those who don't.

But I should add a word of caution. The idea that inventory optimization software can be a silver bullet solution is fool's gold.

What's wrong with inventory optimization of used vehicles?

As I look at the various systems to help dealers and used vehicle managers optimize their inventories, I can only scratch my head.

Inventory optimization is a science and a discipline. As a science, it has certain requirements to make it work. Unfortunately, all of the optimization systems today fail to account for these necessary requirements:

- A lack of statistical relevance. The volumes of used vehicle sales at most dealerships are too small to lend any take-it-to-the-bank insights on what has, can or should sell at a dealership.

- Granular vehicle descriptions. We all know that a particular paint color or accessory can seal the deal on a unit with a given customer. Any optimization system should allow you to plug in these kinds of specifics, on top of mileage, condition, etc. There's at least one system that allows that level of granular detail, but it requires dealers to add the data, which is something that rarely, if ever, gets done.

- Capture of lost sales requests. I'm amazed by some of the vendor claims that a system will help you figure out the units you should stock but don't. The problem: you can't just gauge what you should stock by looking at outside market trends. Lost sales requests are just as important in used vehicles as they are in parts—where managers routinely track the requests to determine the type and number of specific parts they should stock. Without capturing lost sales requests, you fall victim to the trap of not knowing what you could have sold, if you'd only stocked it.

- Rational pricing. Dealers and used vehicle managers often price their vehicles out of the market. An inventory optimization system can tell you exactly what to stock, but unless you base your retail prices on actual market values, and not on what you paid to acquire the vehicle, the data on what sells or doesn't is largely meaningless.

- Market variables. No used vehicle software system can account for the exponential number of market variables—gas prices, interest rates, the weather, an economic slowdown and a host of other factors—that influence customer purchase decisions.

Factor 3: The reality of the Internet

Let's play out a hypothetical: two used vehicle managers each purchase the same make/model unit with the same color/options/mileage at auction for $10,000. Each manager walks away happy; they both believe they're sitting on a unit that could become a home run deal.

Given the acquisition price, each used vehicle manager should be able to mark up the vehicle to $14,000 and potentially get a $4,000 gross profit if the right buyer comes along, correct?

While that seems perfectly reasonable, there's a wild card in today's used vehicle marketplace that makes this scenario, which has worked for decades, much less of a sure-fire thing. In fact, I'd even call the gross profit expectations on this unit a $4,000 Fantasy.

The wild card is the Internet—and only one of the two used vehicle managers in this scenario knows how to use it effectively.

Here's what I mean: the first used manager went back to his dealership, marked up the vehicle to $14,000 and posted the unit on the store's web site and included it in his liner ads. The second used vehicle manager did a little more research. He found that similar units are retailing for about $12,000. So he posted and advertised his unit for $12,500.

When customers are shopping for this vehicle, which used vehicle manager's unit will get noticed?

We all know the answer. The customer is not even going to send an e-mail or call the store with the $14,000 asking price on the unit. The $1,500 price differential is simply too much in today's price-competitive marketplace. In fact, I would bet that the $14,000 price tag just turned the first manager's home run car into a likely candidate for becoming an over-aged unit.

While this is just a hypothetical example, it's a reflection of the dynamics that are occurring online for dealers every day.

Table 1: The Importance of Internet-based Comparative Market Analysis

	Dealer A	Dealer B
Wholesale purchase price	$10,000	$10,000
Internet-based comparative market analysis by dealer?	no	yes
Average retail price of similar units within a 50-mile radius	$12,000	$12,000
Dealer's retail price	$14,000	$12,500
Likelihood of car becoming an over-aged unit	High	Low

"The virtual showroom is becoming the main entrance for most customers," says Cary Donovan, vice president and director of used vehicle operations for Sam Swope Auto Group in Louisville, Kentucky.

That's why Donovan and other dealers are monitoring the prices their competitors offer on vehicles. They don't want to be priced out of the market. These dealers recognize that if they price the vehicle they purchased for $10,000 at $12,000, they'll likely turn the unit more quickly. In their minds, the thinking goes something like this: why wouldn't I sell two or three units for a $2,000 profit in the same time it would take to sell one for a $4,000 gross profit? One of my dealer friends calls this method of efficient operation his "wash, rinse, and repeat" cycle.

The problem for most dealers is that many do not think this way. They have not recognized the profound advantages the Internet has given used vehicle shoppers. Thanks to the availability of pricing guides, it only takes a matter of moments online for today's buyers to develop a short list of dealerships that they'll contact to make a potential purchase. Depending on your retail asking price, you're either in the game or you're not. In some ways, the Internet is "the Great Equalizer" for our business. Few customers today go to a dealer's lot without knowing something about how much a vehicle is worth.

Mitch Golub, president of Cars.com, says only a fraction of dealers have really embraced the new reality of what the Internet means for their used vehicle business. He should know because he sees, every single day, how dealers manage their online inventory and pricing. Of dealers who use Cars.com, only 20 percent are making pricing adjustments multiple times a day to ensure their inventory is competitively positioned for today's price-conscious buyers. These dealers are under-cutting the competition on a daily basis and selling vehicles more quickly and efficiently than their peers.

Who are the dealers that appear to be mastering the medium? "They are often independent dealers in metropolitan markets," Golub says. "A year ago, they didn't know a web site from a chair. But the dealer principals at these stores saw an opportunity for growth and got engaged. When the boss knows it works, everyone else does too. Franchised dealers are still catching up."

THE FUNDAMENTAL KEYS TO INTERNET SUCCESS—PRICING AND POSITIONING

Golub and other pioneering Internet experts believe that proper pricing is one of the fundamental keys to success for selling used vehicles in today's online-influenced marketplace.

"The ability to price-gouge a customer has been reduced by the Internet," says Chip Perry, president of AutoTrader.com, a third-party site many dealerships use to list their used vehicle inventories. Perry adds that dealers who apply traditional mark-ups on vehicles they post online don't do as well as those who are more price-conscious.

"Some dealers believe that all Internet buyers are price-grinding customers," he says. "That's a myth. They are price conscious, but they are not necessarily price-sensitive."

Indeed, Golub's statistics from Cars.com show that for the 80 percent of used vehicle shoppers who use the Internet to hunt for vehicles, price is a chief consideration. These customers may start their shopping process by looking for a type of vehicle that fits their needs. But after they've narrowed the list, vehicle price, mileage and condition are the top drivers that determine whether they'll contact a dealership.

In addition to competitive and realistic pricing, dealers who succeed online also take great pains to properly position vehicles for sale in the online medium. But as Golub and others note, there's a big disconnect between dealers understanding that they need to present vehicles in a compelling way for customers and what they actually do with the inventory they post online.

"There are two types of dealers—those who focus on showcasing the story behind their vehicles and those who are just listing them," Golub says.

Think about Golub's comment for a moment. Earlier in this chapter, we discussed how used vehicles are increasingly becoming like commodities. There are more similar makes and models than ever before, and loyalty to individual brands is less likely to be something that dealers can count on with today's customers.

So what Golub is saying is simply this: while it's true that vehicles are less unique than they used to be, there's still a way for dealers to showcase why a particular vehicle stands out from those to which it is similar.

"A used car is a commodity until it's marketed by a dealer," Golub says. "That's when it's important to tell the story behind each one."

There are a lot of tools dealers can use online to accomplish this ever-important story-telling—vehicle history reports, statements from original owners, research tools on their web site and others.

All of these are important, Golub and others agree, but photographs of your vehicles may be the most important because they can effectively showcase the eye appeal of a vehicle and stop an Internet shopper in his or her tracks.

"Good photographs used to be a nice thing to have," Golub says. "Now they are a must-have on every vehicle."

No one understands this reality more clearly than Cary Donovan at Sam Swope. For him, the presentation of vehicles online is one of the key reasons why the Swope Dealer Group is getting a 1:1 ratio of Internet to traditional showroom customers at its stores.

Donovan calls his online presence his Virtual Showroom and strives to make sure each vehicle looks its best online. "Customers regularly tell us, 'I don't need to see the car, I'll just come in and buy it,'" he says.

Donovan's claim seemed a little strong until I got a better understanding of his strategy. He has set up a studio in a reconditioning center that he and his staff use to take pictures of every used unit they add to inventory. They will take a dozen pictures of each unit—focusing on exactly the same angles (rear, front, side, etc.) and features (odometer, dashboard, etc.) of the vehicle each time. He's even marked the floor to ensure his staff knows where to stand when they take the photographs. On his site, visitors can dial into each photograph or view the entire vehicle as a slide show.

"There's no doubt this has increased our lead generation," Donovan says. "But it didn't come without a lot of blood, sweat and tears to get us to this point. There was a lot of trial and error."

Like many great ideas, Donovan stumbled on to his vision for merchandising his used vehicles online. "When I traveled, I would read magazines like the *Robb Report* and *duPont Registry* and see all these pristine and crisp photographs of yachts and jets that really caught my eye," he says. "I compared that to what we were doing and knew there had to be a better way."

Even Donovan's indoor photo studio resulted from a simple realization. Early on, he was taking photographs outdoors but soon realized the often cloudy and rainy conditions in Louisville didn't provide the pristine backdrop he wanted to achieve.

"The sun doesn't shine as brightly here as it does in Phoenix," he says.

Donovan also recognizes that photos don't tell the whole story about a vehicle. His site also calls out a vehicle's ownership history. For example, about half of his inventory has single owners—a fact he touts on each relevant listing.

Even though the Internet is becoming an increasingly profound force in today's used vehicle business, I still run into long-time industry veterans who simply don't believe it is a powerful sales and marketing tool.

A longtime dealer CPA from the Midwest says, "Joe Six Pack isn't showing up on a dealer's lot with a printout from the Internet."

That may be true in some areas, but most dealers recognize the Internet is a sales and marketing medium that's here to stay, and it'll play an even bigger role in shaping how dealers acquire, price and retail their used vehicle inventories. Currently, AutoTrader.com reports that 12 million buyers pore over its listings each month, and the number of site visitors has been steadily increasing for years.

WHAT THE TRIFECTA OF FACTORY INFLUENCE, THE PROLIFERATION OF USED VEHICLES AND THE REALITY OF THE INTERNET—THE PERFECT STORM—MEANS TO YOU

The message is simply this: between the reality of the Internet and other dynamics, the used vehicle business is more challenging and difficult to manage than it used to be. On one hand, The Perfect Storm is an explanation for why some dealers are having trouble grappling with their inability to build used vehicle volumes and gross profits.

On the other hand, The Perfect Storm analogy is a harbinger of the future: dealers and managers who want to be more successful in today's used vehicle marketplace will need to adopt new ways of investment-minded thinking, new tools and new management skills to achieve the business goals they seek.

A CHANGED MARKET
REQUIRES CHANGED METRICS

I've sat in with dealers and GMs as they conduct job interviews with prospective used vehicle managers. The questions they often ask are predictable and extremely telling.

In these interviews, the dealers and GMs will invariably ask the used vehicle manager candidate about his past accomplishments: the volume of cars the manager and his team delivered on a monthly basis, the average gross profit they were able to achieve and the average age of the used vehicle inventory.

These three metrics—volume, gross and age—are as old as the used vehicle business itself. For nearly 100 years, dealers and used vehicle managers have used these benchmarks to assess the performance of their own used vehicle departments. It's no surprise, then, that these metrics define the job interview with a prospective used vehicle manager.

But here's the thing: these metrics are crude, unreliable and they don't tell the full story of whether the individual manager has done or can do a really good job.

Let's say you have two used vehicle managers, sitting side by side. Each can boast of selling 100 vehicles per month, averaging $2,500 gross profit on each vehicle, and eliminating any inventory 45 days or older. Most dealers, GMs and used vehicle managers would think each of these managers is doing a good job.

But what if the first used vehicle manager posts those numbers with $2.5 million in inventory, and the second gets the same results with $1 million in inventory? Knowing that, who's doing a better job now?

I think all of us would agree that the second manager is doing better. He's tying up less cash and selling units far more efficiently than the other manager. There's a term for this kind of retailing and profit-making efficiency: velocity.

Table 2: Velocity = less cash outlay, more car sales

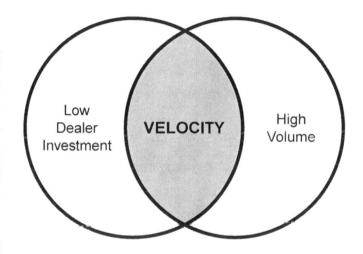

But the problem for many dealers and used vehicle managers today is that they haven't been trained to operate with investment-minded benchmarks like equity position and velocity. Simply put, most are not trained to look under the hood of used vehicle departments—either when they're interviewing a candidate or managing their own used vehicle department.

I'm not saying that these age-old metrics—volume, gross profit, and age—don't matter. They do. But they are only part of the equation that results in profitable success for today's used vehicle departments.

Dealers and used vehicle managers today need to be more astute about their used vehicle department's financial performance, using what I call the vital signs of their inventory investment on a daily basis. I say vital signs because I liken the way a used vehicle manager should evaluate a department to the way a physician or a nurse gauges the health of a patient.

Medical professionals routinely check a patient's blood pressure, heart rate and pulse to monitor their condition and discern changes that would signal improving or weakening health. It should be true for dealers and used vehicle managers.

Why is this so important? It's because the used vehicle inventory is the single largest asset most dealerships own, outside of any land and buildings. It's often a seven-figure investment and, unlike most investments, it depreciates every day. It seems this type of investment deserves the same kind of careful, ongoing oversight and skill that a doctor or nurse would give to a patient.

To put this thinking into financial terms, your used vehicle inventory requires the same skills and attention that an astute financial advisor would apply to the individual portfolios he manages. A dealer's used inventory is an investment. It ties up money. It's fair to say that without applying a more telling set of vital signs to the health of this investment, you're probably not making the return you could—and you might be taking a bath.

THE VITAL SIGNS

1. **Total units in stock and total inventory investment.** Whenever I ask a used vehicle manager to relay the total units in stock and the total value of his inventory, the first word out the manager's mouth is "about." He's estimating both figures. I wonder: if your doctor told you your blood pressure was "about" 140/80, would you be satisfied? The answer is probably no. Today's managers should know, first-hand, what's sitting on their lots. These figures are an all-important starting point to drilling down into the financial health of a used vehicle inventory.

2. **Average investment on an inventory-wide basis.** Tommy Gibbs, a successful Toyota dealer in Chesapeake, Virginia and a highly regarded used vehicle consultant, preaches this point as gospel. We both believe that this figure should be in every used vehicle manager's brain, 24/7/365. As Gibbs

puts it, the knowledge helps his used vehicle managers adjust to changing market conditions—such as factory incentive programs that erode used vehicle values or an up-tick in interest rates. His used vehicle managers know, to the dime, whether their average inventory investment is $8,500 or $10,000 at any moment, and they can give you good, rational reasons for why it's higher one month, and lower the next.

Gibbs knows that a lower average unit cost delivers two important results: it reduces his risk of losses due to value and price fluctuations, and it effectively guarantees his managers are buying inventory that offers a value difference for buyers, who might otherwise step up to a new unit if given the opportunity.

In my experience, most used vehicle managers simply aren't aware of their average inventory investment. In today's market, that's a cardinal sin. This knowledge should guide just about every decision a used manager makes about a vehicle, from acquisition to disposition.

What would you do if you learned that the financial advisor managing your personal financial portfolio made decisions about what to buy or sell without fully understanding how much you've invested in the stocks you owned? I suspect you'd be looking for a different advisor.

3. **Your equity position for your inventory and individual vehicles.** I laugh when I think about the old saying, "it pays to own a car right." Everyone in this business understands that statement. It's the reason we're in the business. When you buy right, vehicles sell faster and grosses, as well as commission checks, are higher.

So no one argues that buying right for a used vehicle, whether it's through a trade or at auction, is probably the single-best thing we can do to ensure a better return on the money we've invested in the vehicle. In effect, this statement says that the equity or investment you've got in a vehicle really truly matters—possibly more than anything else.

But here's the irony that makes me chuckle: despite the understanding that a vehicle's equity position is important, it's rarely, if ever, heeded in the day-to-day hurly-burly of dealers' used vehicle departments. It's not something that is top of mind, and it's not something that used vehicle managers and dealers put into practice from a management perspective. Few used vehicle managers could look at a vehicle and truly know its prospects for making a return. They might have a gut feel, but that doesn't cut it anymore in today's marketplace.

More than anything else, the used vehicle manager's job is managing the dealer's investment in inventory. It seems mighty apparent that understanding the equity position of each vehicle would be critically important to managing the likelihood that their overall inventory will deliver a healthy return for their dealer.

Let's go back to the financial advisor analogy: would you want someone making decisions on selling your stocks without knowing how much you paid for them and understanding, with certainty, that a decision to sell is either going to bring you a return or reduce your risk of loss?

Understanding the equity position of your vehicles in inventory—knowing how much you stand to gain or lose when you sell it for a given price—can be a powerful tool for dealers and used vehicle managers. For starters, it's a sure-fire way to know when a vehicle's about to show water, enabling you to take steps to prevent a wholesale loss.

Can you see where this is going? In time, the power of managing your used vehicle investment compounds its positive benefits, just like interest on a loan.

Dealers and used vehicle managers who understand the "equity in inventory concept" become more efficient at knowing what to buy, how much they should pay, what price they should ask at retail and when they should take quick steps to retail or wholesale their way out of a potential problem.

Remember Jerrod Musser, the former stockbroker who oversees used vehicle operations at a Colorado Ford store? He's monitoring vehicle scores and getting rid of vehicles at 5, 10 and 15 days into their life cycles because he knows they can't make the return on investment he expects.

Compared with other dealers and used vehicle managers who aren't applying such a disciplined approach, who do you think is going to be more competitive and profitable?

4. **The average turn of your inventory.** By average turn, I'm not talking about a turn policy of 30, 45 or 60 days. No, I want to know how many times the inventory has turned in a given year.

A store that can turn its inventory more quickly invariably makes more money, takes fewer wholesale losses and, more than likely, does it with less cash tied up in inventory costs. That's velocity. In essence, a faster turn reduces the risks that daily depreciation and other market changes will harm a dealer's inventory investment.

> *A store that can turn its inventory more quickly invariably makes more money, takes fewer wholesale losses and, more than likely, does it with less cash tied up in inventory costs. That's velocity. In essence, a faster turn reduces the risks that daily depreciation and other market changes will harm a dealer's inventory investment.*

Here's an example: Tom Shirey turns his inventory of 80-plus vehicles nearly 15 times a year. By focusing on turn, he's got no choice but to put his emphasis on vehicles that move the quickest. "It's like a religion for us," Shirey says. He is also able to achieve this impressive turn rate with an average total inventory value that's about 40 percent less than his inventory investment from prior years.

Gary Duncan laughs when he talks about turn rate. "Some guys are old school," he says. "They've got $2.5 million in used vehicle inventory and only sell 40 vehicles a month. I've got $1.2 million in inventory and I'm selling 80 units a month."

At present, our used vehicle business lacks a consistent understanding of what turn means and how to measure it. But guess what? You already have an expert on turn in your stores—it's your parts manager.

I'll bet you dollars to donuts that your parts manager can tell you what inventory turn and velocity mean—and he or she can probably drill it down to show you data on a retail and wholesale basis, all the way down to individual parts.

The irony of this shouldn't escape you. Most parts managers apply a greater level of inventory management sophistication to an investment that's more predictable than used vehicles—and, in many cases, probably one-eighth the size. What makes the irony even more apparent and painful is that parts managers are not dealing with an investment that's as volatile as used vehicles. Depreciation occurs every day in used vehicles, whether you write it down or not. By contrast, parts managers don't have to wrestle with depreciation. In fact, the value of their inventory tends to go up, not down.

Table 3: Inventory Vital Signs

Sign	Importance
Total number of units in stock, average investment per vehicle, and total investment dollars	These figures are the starting point for drilling down into the financial health of a used vehicle inventory.
Equity position on entire inventory as well as on a car by car basis	Dealers who understand this become more efficient at knowing what to buy, how much they should pay, what price they should ask at retail, and when they should take quick steps to retail or wholesale their way out of a potential problem.
Average turn	A store that can turn its inventory more quickly makes more money, takes fewer wholesale losses and does it with less cash tied up in inventory. A faster turn also reduces the risks from depreciation and other market changes.

The application of used vehicle Vital Signs

I've shared these inventory vital signs for two reasons.

First, I want to give dealers and used vehicle managers a firm elbow nudge: there's a better, more financially sound way of managing your used vehicle business to achieve improved sales volume and profits.

Rest assured, I'm not chastising anyone for not using this approach before. As I mentioned earlier, the used vehicle business has been forgiving and none of us really needed to worry about anything beyond the time-tested metrics of volume, gross and age.

Today's more challenging used vehicle marketplace requires more management sophistication and greater attention to improving dealers' investments in their used vehicle inventories, and growing sales volume and profits. Such gains are attainable with the right investment-minded attitude, people and approach.

But, today's more challenging used vehicle marketplace requires more management sophistication and greater attention to improving dealers' investments in their used vehicle inventories, and growing sales volume and profits. Such gains are attainable with the right investment-minded attitude, people and approach.

Second, the vital signs serve as a framework for the remainder of the book. In subsequent chapters, I show how the awareness of these vital signs can make remarkable differences in the way used vehicle managers go about their daily work of pricing, appraising, acquiring, reconditioning and desking used vehicles.

As you might expect, you'll also see how the application of these vital signs can transform sales volumes and profits at virtually any dealership's used vehicle operation, irrespective of franchise or location.

THE CHOCOLATE
CAKE FACTOR

I've got a voracious sweet tooth, which means it's hard for me to refuse a second piece of chocolate cake when it's offered to me.

But I'll likely refuse it for a simple reason: I know that my body's metabolism can burn off the first piece with little trouble. In that way, I'm lucky. I can eat a piece of cake whenever I want to, and I don't worry about the effects it has on my waistline. I also know, however, that a second or third piece is pushing it for me.

It takes a fair amount of discipline to say no thanks to those second or third pieces of cake. But that's what I do, because I'm aware of my metabolism and understand my limits.

What on earth does chocolate cake have to do with used cars? In the last chapter, I shared the vital signs that are essential for any dealer or used vehicle manager to successfully incorporate an investment-minded approach to managing their used vehicle inventories. By monitoring these vital signs, just as a doctor would monitor the vital signs of a patient, you can glean important clues about the health and vitality of the investments (vehicles) that are sitting in your inventory. The vital signs will tell you whether a vehicle's destined for a sizable or short gross profit, or whether it's a dog that you'd better wholesale to minimize a loss.

In some ways, the vital signs are the window you can use to view and shape the metabolism of your used vehicle department. I know that if I exercised more, my metabolism would be better able to burn off that second or third piece of chocolate cake that my sweet tooth wants to enjoy.

THE METABOLISM OF YOUR USED VEHICLE DEPARTMENT

The same is true of the metabolism of your used vehicle department and inventory. On any given day, a used vehicle manager will, knowingly or not, stretch on a trade appraisal or pay above book value to help close new vehicle deals or fill gaps in inventory—essentially the equivalent of eating that second or third piece of chocolate cake.

Tom Shirey has a used vehicle department with the metabolism of someone who runs five miles a day, every day of the week. His department can afford to stretch on a trade appraisal to do a deal or pay above book at auction. Why? It's because his department is powered by the daily exercise of maintaining a disciplined turn rate and monitoring the equity position for each vehicle. In the end, his department can handle the second or third piece of chocolate cake without consequence.

As a result, Shirey can afford to be more aggressive on purchasing inventory and setting appraisals. In fact, I would assert that Shirey, and other dealers who apply investment management principles to their used vehicle departments, actually *deserve* to be aggressive because they've created a metabolism that allows them to be that way.

The discipline of following investment-minded management principles allows you to reward yourself once in a while, as does the discipline of working out every day.

Financial advisors know this is true. If an investment advisor has wisely managed the returns on a portfolio, he may well decide that he can afford to take a more aggressive posture in his buying and selling decisions because his disciplined approach to managing the portfolio enables him to take on the additional risk.

To me, that's the beauty of applying investment-minded management principles to the used vehicle department. Not only does the data you glean from understanding and monitoring your inventory's vital signs give you a more solid financial basis for managing your inventory, it lets you choose to be the type of manager you want to be. If you want to be aggressive, you can be. If you prefer to be conservative, that's okay, too.

It's easy to spot dealers and used vehicle managers who use investment-minded principles for managing their departments. They're often wholesaling vehicles that other dealers would consider too "fresh" to get rid of, or they're offering rock-bottom prices (and taking short, $1,000 deals) right out of the gate to turn the units they acquire. They do this because they know some units can be troubled, investment-wise, from day one.

The flip-side is also true. When these dealers acquire a vehicle back of book, they can aim for maximum gross profits right out of the gate. They know they have a longer window of opportunity to sell it before age and depreciation start to erode their positive equity position and harm the potential investment return.

Other dealers, meanwhile, continue to mark up units with the $4,000 Fantasy in mind, and often don't understand why they continue to have an age problem in their used vehicle department.

When you apply investment-based, equity-minded management principles you can have that second and third piece of chocolate cake—and make money every time you do.

PRICING TO MARKET

"Your name isn't Dale. It's Santa!"

This comment came from a dealer with whom I shared a used vehicle pricing tool that my company, vAuto, had developed. This enthusiasm came from the recognition that this tool will virtually guarantee leads on every vehicle, make their vehicles more price competitive and help eliminate any wholesale losses.

Bold claims, you think?

Take a look at CarMax. They're making truckloads of profits because they have figured out a way to purchase and price their vehicles more competitively and efficiently than anyone else. You readers who compete directly with CarMax outlets know exactly what I'm talking about. You know what it's like to see someone else consistently sell vehicles at lower prices and somehow manage to stay profitable and in business.

Of course, there's more to CarMax's success than just how they purchase and price their used vehicles. But we can all agree their processes are a lot less emotional and far more data-driven than those that dealers and used vehicle managers claim to follow. Or, to put it another way, they don't purchase and price their vehicles the way most dealers and used vehicle managers have done for years.

THE LET'S GET LUCKY GAME

One of my good friends and financial advisors is Anthony Richards. He's a managing principal at his own Chicago-area brokerage firm, Stairway Partners. Richards used to manage an $85 billion institutional investment fund for a national financial house. He retired in his 40s and has since started his own brokerage company.

I'd gone to Richards to improve my understanding of how commodities traders make their money.

Richards' business intrigues me because I believe that the kind of investment-minded principles he applies to managing portfolios mirrors the approach that dealers and used vehicle managers must adopt to ensure their used vehicle departments can remain competitive and profitable in the coming years.

I shared with Richards the approach most dealers and used vehicle managers apply to the pricing of their vehicles. For most, it starts with their actual cash value (ACV) or the money they've invested in a vehicle. From there, it's typically a standard mark-up of $3,000 to $5,000.

"That sounds wishful," Richards interjects.

"It is," I say.

"But how do the dealers really know what the market will bear? The pricing doesn't seem to relate to true market value. You can't be off the market and compete. Seems to me that's a really risky thing to do with the dealer's money," he adds.

"I know. But that's how it's done. That's how we did it when I was a dealer. It's like we all want to get lucky and get the margin we think we want and need."

Our conversation continued, covering how dealers and used vehicle managers appraise and purchase vehicles, how they make decisions to recondition and what little, if any, attention is typically given to the health of individual investments in vehicles for the weeks of their life cycle in a dealer's inventory.

"Everything is so ad hoc," he says. "It seems such an inefficient use of dealers' capital."

His comment hit like a bolt of lightning. In Richards' world of buying and selling commodities and other investments, there's little, if any, wishful thinking. He uses an objective, data-rich process to determine the risk factors for any investment and its potential returns. When he decides to sell, it's based on a keen, data-driven understanding of the markets and their prevailing prices.

It's not difficult to figure out why these objective, data-fueled processes are important for Richards. In the markets in which he works, margins are razor thin. Plus, everybody's watching his performance.

PRICING EFFICIENCY AND OPERATIONAL EFFICIENCY

As I gained a deeper appreciation for Richards' business, I couldn't help but think how far off many dealers and used vehicle managers are from his breed of investment-minded thinking. Richards articulated two key objectives for his work, which I believe are an ideal foundation for the goals dealers and used vehicle managers should apply to their inventories. The two goals:

- Pricing efficiency: In lay terms, this is simply knowing the price point at which the item you have to sell is both appealing and competitive to would-be buyers and can deliver the return on investment you want to achieve. Pricing efficiency also means you know the precise point at which you'd better sell to minimize additional risk and potential losses. There's another term for this two-way principle, "pricing to market."

- Operational efficiency: Very few decisions that Richards makes are done without the benefit of market data (potential risk, price points, past ROI performance, etc.). He doesn't make guesses or assumptions. Instead, he consistently follows the same process of assessing and quantifying risk for a given investment, determining the prospective return, and calculating how long it may take to achieve his desired return. The discipline means he makes fewer costly mistakes, and he makes more money as a result.

Imagine what improvements your used vehicle department could make if you got in the habit of using pricing and operational efficiencies as the foundation for your used vehicle department. The outcome is pretty clear: you'd make money faster on the units you know you can sell and you'd lose less (if any) money on the ones that don't.

"The key is you need to have objective information and a clear, consistent process evaluating your potential risk and return," Richards says.

You may be thinking: "That's great, Dale. But how do I apply what Tony's saying to my used vehicle operations? The kind of pricing and sales history data he's using simply doesn't exist."

Friends, I'm here to tell you that the data does exist, and there are tools available today that you can use to take a more astute, investment-minded approach to your used vehicle operations. Like any savvy financial advisor, you can use these tools to purchase your used vehicles with an expected return on investment in mind and, similarly, to price your vehicles to offer

the most competitive carrot to would-be buyers and
deliver the gross profit returns you expect.

THE POWER OF A DATA-FUELED
PRICING TOOL

The purpose of this chapter is to help you understand
and achieve the type of pricing efficiencies that
financial wizards like Richards dutifully achieve every
day. The idea of pricing efficiency is not new. Big Box
retailers like Wal-Mart have deployed this idea for
years with great success.

In the auto business, however, pricing to market is a
relatively new concept.

In terms of pricing, we already know that most
dealers will use their ACV or the price paid for a used
unit as a starting point to set a retail asking price.
We've also established that, for the most part, the
mark-ups dealers and used vehicle managers put on
vehicles is arbitrary—the $4,000 Fantasy in action.
Such price-setting is based solely on the price they've
paid for a vehicle and not on what the potential
market will give in return for the investment.

Let's play out this scenario. You purchase a vehicle
for $10,000, set a retail asking price of $15,000 and

put it on your front line. What happens next? At many stores, the answer is virtually nothing—until the vehicle hits 30, 45, 60 or even 90 days in inventory. It's at that point, when someone realizes a vehicle may have a problem, that you begin to look at adjusting pricing and trying to improve the unit's retail sales prospects.

In my view, that's an incredibly inefficient approach. Yet this is a common practice in our industry.

If you wait 30 days to pay any attention to a vehicle's sales prospects or retail positioning, you've lost a full month's worth of opportunity to turn the investment you've got in the vehicle into a return. As Richards suggests, this would be an inefficient use of a dealer's money. The problem only gets worse if the inattention extends to 45, 60 or even 90 days, which it does at many stores I visit.

The combination of pricing inefficiency and inattention to a unit's investment status creates even more trouble when you pay too much for a unit from the get-go (a necessary thing, sometimes, to make a new deal fly). In these instances, dealers who apply their customary mark-ups have exponentially increased the chances for a wholesale loss. In fact, I'd assert that such vehicles were destined to be wholesal losers from day one, thanks to inefficient pricing and inattention to the unit's prospects.

On top of all this, many dealers add a "pack" to their used vehicle pricing. Packs have a detrimental effect on a vehicle's salability. Remember my earlier point about today's buyers: they've got a firmer handle on pricing than they've ever had before—and they can likely find a vehicle that's similar to the one you're offering. The addition of a pack, on top of an "Up from ACV" approach to pricing, are key reasons why many dealers watch their used vehicles become wholesale problems.

Today's used vehicle marketplace requires more skill and sophistication when it comes to pricing and establishing gross profit targets than simply marking up a unit (pack and all) and hoping that you might "get lucky" on a car. This is not the most efficient or wise way to achieve a respectable return on your used vehicle inventory investment.

There's no mystery as to why this common approach to pricing used vehicles occurs: it goes back to the belief that a solid, gross profit-generating deal will eventually come around. There's nothing wrong with the desire and impulse to make the best profit return or gross profit on your vehicle.

But today's used vehicle marketplace requires more skill and sophistication when it comes to pricing and establishing gross profit targets than simply marking up a unit (pack and all) and hoping that you might "get lucky" on a car. This is not the most efficient or wise way to achieve a respectable return on your used vehicle inventory investment.

Enter the pricing tool developed at vAuto. This is the tool that has one dealer referring to me as Santa. I believe that this will be a significant, industry-changing force for franchised dealers.

A LOOK UNDER THE HOOD OF vAUTO'S PRICING TOOL

The vAuto pricing tool will be disruptive because it provides, for the first time in the automotive industry, a reliable gauge to help used vehicle managers set retail asking prices with the full knowledge of how their decision will play out in a given market.

Imagine a dashboard on your computer screen with a tachometer and several individual fields that contain data about a given vehicle. The fields show information about the specific vehicle—year, make, condition, mileage, equipment, options, and the like. In addition, the fields detail how much you've paid for the vehicle, the number of days it's been in your inventory and the amount of gross profit you can expect, given the retail asking price you set for the unit.

As you set your retail asking price, the tool automatically shows you how a specific vehicle compares with similar units at other dealerships— what we call the vehicle's competitive positioning or rank in the marketplace. We already know that consumers effectively value rank vehicles when they shop, using price, condition and other variables. So why not adopt a similar approach in our used vehicle departments?

Let's play out this functionality with a real-life example. A Chevrolet store had a 2003 Ford Ranger priced at $14,475. The vAuto pricing tool shows that the vehicle, at its current pricing, was ranked 10th out of 13 other similar models available at dealerships within a 50-mile radius.

If we were to raise the asking price by $200, the ranking would move to 11th out of 13. Likewise, if we lowered the asking price by $200, it wouldn't change the vehicle's competitive ranking at all—it stays at 11 out of 13. If we move the price downward by $500, the vehicle moves to 7th position.

At the same time, the pricing tool shows what effect these possible adjustments to the vehicle price will have on the gross profit the vehicle may generate. By moving the price up, the gross profit improves; by moving it down, the gross profit gets smaller.

Table 4: The Pricing Tool

	Scenario A	Scenario B	Scenario C
2003 Ford Ranger Retail Price	$14,475	$14,675	$13,975
Price Adjustment	$0	$200	<$500>
Rank versus identically, equipped vehicles within a 50-mile radius of the dealership	10/13	11/13	7/13

Can you see why dealers who have seen this tool, which is similar to the kinds of software my financial friend uses, think it's so powerful?

When I talk about this tool with dealers, I'll often bet them that the vast majority of their inventory is far less competitive in their marketplace than they think it is. I then take the next step and plug a dealers' inventory into the vAuto pricing tool and display the competitive rankings. These dealers invariably have what can only be described as an "Aha!" moment.

Dealers who are using the vAuto pricing tool say it delivers several key benefits:

- It delivers a better sense of competitive positioning. The vAuto pricing tool replaces the newspaper and Internet scans of used units at competing stores that some dealers and used vehicle managers use to get a pulse on their markets. I'd guess that only a minority of dealerships actually uses this crude and rudimentary measuring stick in any formative way. vAuto's technology, which scans Internet offerings of competing inventory to provide its competitive ranking intelligence, is a far more efficient way to assess how a given price on a vehicle stacks up to its competition. It's as simple as moving the dial on your dashboard.

- It lets you maximize your gross profit potential. In the case of the '03 Ranger, we could make pricing adjustments and know the exact dollar amount at which the Ranger falls to a lower rung on the competitive ladder, or moves up, depending on whether you raise or lower your price. It does this while telling you how these changes would affect the gross profits you'd get if you sold the unit. Smart dealers who use the tool are quick to recognize and then rectify an inefficient pricing habit that's prevalent at most dealerships: vehicles are typically priced in $500 increments.

Guess what'll happen if you price your vehicle at $200 or $300 increments using the vAuto tool? Your vehicles will be more attractive to price-sensitive buyers because you've exploited the wiggle room in the marketplace pricing. With the vAuto tool, you can figure out exactly what price will make your vehicles more competitive and not lose any gross profit potential.

One last question: what effect do you think this smarter, more finite approach to pricing will have, given weeks and months' worth of deals, on your dealership's showroom traffic, volume and gross profits?

- It will help ferret out potential wholesale losses. The pricing tool shows you if you've paid too much for a vehicle, based on the vAuto system's checks of auction and value guide prices. You'll know right away if a vehicle is troubled from an investment perspective as well as how to price the unit so it can be competitive right away—or eliminated to avoid a future problem.

Remember Tom Shirey's comment about dumping a fresh car if, in his estimation, it won't make money? That's the kind of power the vAuto pricing tool delivers. The converse is also true: on some units, you have to be price-aggressive right out of the gate if you're in too deep and hope to make any money at will.

In these instances, the vAuto system effectively stops you from applying a random mark-up that will make the vehicle uncompetitive and leave you, 30 or 45 days later, wondering why you're looking at a potential wholesale problem. You stand a far better chance of retailing these units— and making some money—if you price them correctly right away.

- It tells you how long it will take for a vehicle to sell. Part of the behind the scenes technology the vAuto system uses is a three-point review of all used vehicles in a given market place. The system measures when they first appear, along with the initial pricing. Next, the system logs any pricing changes that occur in the vehicle's lifecycle. Finally, the system tracks when a vehicle goes away or gets sold. The system makes these measurements for your inventory and all other competing inventories.

- By tracking variables in vehicle lifecycles, we can predict how long a given vehicle (including its make, configurations, etc.) will typically remain in inventory at any given price point before it sells. This is a critical tool dealers and used vehicle managers can use to more properly project their expected returns on their investments and make more astute decisions about what additional inventory they may need and when they may need it.

> *By tracking variables in vehicle lifecycles, we can predict how long a given vehicle (including its make, configurations, etc.) will typically remain in inventory at any given price point before it sells. This is a critical tool dealers and used vehicle managers can use to more properly project their expected returns on their investments and make more astute decisions about what additional inventory they may need and when they may need it.*

- It lets you desk deals more intelligently. One team of early adopters who are using the vAuto tool applies it as a gut-check when they're about to desk a deal. Before they make an offer to acquire a used vehicle, the dealership managers use the tool to make sure their deals are in line with market dynamics. I'm told that this has helped them add additional gross, and avoid insulting price-savvy customers, when they desk deals.

It won't come easy for dealers and used vehicle managers to embrace this type of pricing and operational efficiency. The lure of a big gross profit deal is just too strong.

One of my favorite general managers who is intimately involved with used vehicles is Yury Ablin. He's smart enough to see why a pricing tool would help eliminate the pricing and operational inefficiencies that he knows exist in his used vehicle department.

But he can't resist the urge to set a price that he thinks he can get, irrespective of knowing whether it's truly competitive or not. For him, the lure of a sizable gross profit on a deal is too strong.

"I'm a fighter," he says. "I'm not convinced I can't get the price I want. I have to give it a chance, but I'll only do it for a while."

I respect Ablin's position. He, like anyone, deserves to give the vehicle a shot at yielding a sizable gross profit. But he's smart enough to hedge his bet, and pull the plug on his initial pricing if he isn't getting any nibbles.

A realization: Competitive pricing hurts without proper purchasing

Because the vAuto pricing tool is based on objective, live market data, it often exposes some of the trouble spots that occur every day in dealers' used vehicle departments.

I've had several conversations with dealers who, after we've plugged their units into the pricing tool, have realized that they can't make any money when they make their pricing more competitive. Often, the problem goes back to the way they acquired the vehicle in the first place.

For example, a dealer and I recently examined a used 2006 Chevrolet Cobalt that he had purchased 18 days earlier. The dealer had priced the unit at $17,990 and the pricing tool showed its competitive ranking was 37th out of 41 similar vehicles, a position that would virtually assure no takers. The tool also showed that asking this price would yield a gross profit of $2,800.

The dealer then asked what would happen if he made the car more competitive and placed it 10th among the rankings of similar vehicles, a position that we both agreed would likely drive traffic. We adjusted the ranking to 10th and found we would have to adjust our asking price to $14,767. Then came the kicker: the gross profit dropped to -$423.

"I can't make any money doing this," the dealer says.

"Of course," I reply. "That's because you never purchased the vehicle right in the first place. What do you expect?"

The dealer immediately understood the linkage: smart, savvy and data-fueled pricing—and the gross profits you can achieve by using tools like vAuto's— work best when you purchase vehicles on the money and understand how acquisition prices create a direct, downstream impact on the gross profits you can expect to make.

Table 5: Why Dealer Acquisition Price Matters

	Scenario A	Scenario B
2006 Chevy Cobalt Retail Price	$17,990	$14,767
Rank versus identically equipped vehicles within a 50-mile radius of the dealership	37/41	10/41
Gross profit	$2,800	$-423

Applying Investment Principles to Used Vehicle Acquisitions

Gary Duncan uses what he calls a "bullpen" when it comes to appraising potential trade-in vehicles. His managers from both new and used departments confer on every vehicle to determine what price they should offer a customer.

"We want to make sure we adjust for the market and make sure the cars we take in are on the money," Duncan says. "It's got everybody focused and, over time, it's going to help us get more trades."

On the surface, it may seem like a pretty simple strategy. Like many dealers, Duncan's hungry for quality used vehicle inventory. He knows, like most dealers, that his best shot at acquiring inventory on the money occurs during the appraisal process, and not through lucky, back-of-book buys at an auction.

But there's a lot more going on beneath the surface that makes the approach Duncan uses for appraisals a sound example of what happens when a dealership deploys a more investment-minded process to its acquisition of used vehicle inventory.

In essence, what Duncan and his managers are doing is double-checking to make sure that they don't pay too much for a unit and that they give the vehicle its best possible chance to make the gross profit returns Duncan wants to generate from his investment. They are making sure that the equity position of the vehicle is strong from the get-go.

The bullpen conversation also has another key benefit. Duncan and his managers recognize that if they step up on an appraisal, they are adding costs and risk into the equation that may dampen the investment's equity position and its potential returns. The conversation is also a precursor to determining how best to price the unit so that it has the best possible chance of delivering a satisfactory gross profit rather than becoming a future wholesale loss.

At too many dealerships there is little, if any, discussion on par with the dialogue that Duncan and his managers share as they acquire vehicles through appraisals. For most stores, the focus rests solely on setting an appraisal number that will close a deal. There's little recognition of the downstream effects these appraisal decisions—particularly those that require stepping up to help the new vehicle department—have on the equity position of the store's investment.

There's a far better way for dealers and used vehicle managers to acquire their used inventory.

This new approach applies both to used vehicle inventory that you acquire through trade-in appraisals or auctions. It's an approach that lets dealers and used vehicle managers clearly see the effects their acquisition decisions will have on a unit's likelihood to sell at retail quickly and the unit's propensity to generate a return on investment. In fact, this approach lets you know, from the first day a vehicle is in inventory, whether you've got a retail winner or a wholesale loser on your hands. In addition, this approach will even tell you how long you can keep a vehicle in inventory before it starts to cost you money.

The foundation for this approach is the kind of investment-minded discussion that Duncan and his managers have when they talk about appraisals. This chapter focuses on acquiring vehicles through trade-in appraisals because it is the single-most efficient way for a dealership to acquire used inventory on the money.

I'm not suggesting that auctions and other wholesale sources for vehicles are not important. They are, and the same type of investment-fueled thinking should apply to any vehicle you purchase at auction. However, trade-ins offer the best opportunity for a dealership to acquire a vehicle at the best possible price.

It's also important to focus on appraisals because of the innate tension that they generate between the new and used vehicle departments. I see this tension, time and again, effectively causing dealers and used vehicle managers to shoot themselves in the foot when they take in trades.

It doesn't have to be this way, and this chapter will show you how a balanced, investment-minded approach to acquiring used vehicles makes everyone in your dealership a winner, particularly dealers, who will enjoy an improved return on their investments.

ACKNOWLEDGING THE TRUTH: APPRAISALS DESERVE MORE SCRUTINY

In my role as president of vAuto, I spend much of my time visiting dealerships. As I travel across the country, I see dozens of dealerships where dealers and used vehicle managers nod their heads in agreement that yes, the trade-in is our best opportunity to buy vehicles right ... no question about it.

But then I'll ask the question that often brings an uneasy silence: what do you do to manage your appraisal process and how do you know whether you're doing a good job at it?

The reality at many stores is that while appraisals are the single-most important way to ensure that you're buying a vehicle at the right price and giving it the best shot at generating a return, it also represents the least-managed component in your entire sales process.

Here's what I mean. If I asked you how many TOs, deliveries or demo drives occurred at your store yesterday or the day before, you'd be able to tell me (or at least you have the tools that should enable you to do so). The same, unfortunately, cannot be said about appraisals.

In most of the stores I visit, the appraisal process
resembles The Wild West. It's not uncommon to
have used vehicle managers, sales managers, assistant
managers, GMs and salespeople all taking a hand
in appraising vehicles. Few stores deploy metrics
to determine who's effective or ineffective at this
important practice, and even fewer actually manage
the data they gather about appraisals.

With a backdrop like this, how does anyone know
whether the appraisals conducted are poor, good or
outstanding? The fact is, you can't reliably answer
these questions unless you've actually taken the time
to ask them in the first place and develop a system
to measure the effect your appraisals have *every day*
on your ability to make a sound, profit-generating
investment decision on a used vehicle.

Most dealers can't afford to let this part of their
business go untended and unmanaged any longer.

If you're at a domestic store, chances are you're
having a harder time attracting customers to come
in to buy a new vehicle. That, of course, means you
have fewer opportunities to appraise and acquire
trade-ins for your used vehicle department. The
flypaper effect of your brand—that is, its stickiness
to attract customers—has diminished, as has what

was once a reliable pipeline of vehicles for your used vehicle department.

This is a key reason why more and more used vehicle managers at domestic stores spend a greater portion of their time at online and traditional auctions to acquire used vehicles. This is a less cost-effective way to acquire inventory, but few dealers and used vehicle managers take the next, important step of exploring how to *do* a better job of retaining the vehicles that do present themselves as potential trade-ins.

INJECTING BALANCE IN THE APPRAISAL PROCESS

The first step in improving your appraisal process is to acknowledge the reality that appraisals serve two masters, your new *and* your used vehicle departments.

Too often, appraisals are just a tool that serves the new vehicle department at the expense of the used vehicle department.

Here's what I mean: you value a $10,000 vehicle at $12,000 to complete a new vehicle deal, you've just added $2,000 in acquisition costs to the vehicle for your used vehicle department. What effect do you think this will have on the ability of your used vehicle manager to achieve a respectable gross profit? The answer is that you've just made it far more difficult to achieve a healthy return and, in many cases, you've probably ensured that the vehicle is destined to become an aged unit.

Here's an exercise that always opens eyes when I share it with dealers and used vehicle managers: take a look at the vehicles your used department has recently wholesaled because they reached 45 or 60 days in your inventory. How many of those vehicles started with a too-high appraisal that enabled you to close a new vehicle deal—and then forced the used vehicle manager to elevate the retail asking price to make up for added baggage that your appraisal created? If your store is like most, you'll find a sizable share of those wholesale units fall into this category.

Are you thinking: but how will I be able to sell my new units if I can't use the trade-in as another way to add leg into our new vehicle gross profits?

The answer to this question lies in the way you think about appraisals and how you use them in a more balanced fashion to serve the needs of both your new and used vehicle departments.

The balanced approach to appraisals that I advocate calls for more up-front recognition that appraisals truly affect the fortunes of both your new and used vehicle departments and that every person who handles an appraisal needs to be aware of which department needs the most assistance on any given day. Appraisals really serve two broad purposes:

1. Make the deal for the new vehicle department

2. Properly set up a future deal for the used vehicle department

This is the mindset that Gary Duncan's managers bring to the bullpen when they discuss appraisals. They understand it's a balancing act, similar to a two-person dance where each partner moves in tandem with the other. This way they can keep both departments happy and profitable.

On some days, it may be necessary to step up on an appraisal. When I was a dealer, I had this discussion many times with my used vehicle manager. We did this because we had a slow month and needed to juice up our new vehicle volumes.

I would add that we were also lucky. Fifteen years ago, we could get away with stepping up on appraisals because the used vehicle business was more forgiving. Buyers were willing to pay the added acquisition costs we baked into our retail asking prices.

But in today's market, where consumers are much more price-sensitive, it's far more challenging to bury those additional acquisition costs in your retail asking price and achieve the necessary return on investment a used department requires to be profitable.

Did you catch the nuance in that last sentence? I said it was "far more challenging" to bury the additional, appraisal-triggered acquisition costs into your retail asking prices for your used vehicles. I didn't say it was impossible to do so.

HOW APPRAISAL SCORES BALANCE THE NEEDS OF USED AND NEW VEHICLE DEPARTMENTS

When Gary Duncan's managers sit down to discuss appraisals in their bullpen, they're using an appraisal score sheet that's part of the vAuto system. It gives them a data-rich analysis on every appraisal.

The score tells Duncan and his managers the effect that any appraisal will have on the future fortunes of a particular used vehicle. If they've over-allowed on an appraisal to secure a new vehicle deal, the score tells them how much that additional acquisition cost will eat into the potential future gross profits (or investment return) the vehicle is likely to generate.

Similarly, if they managed to appraise a vehicle back of book, the score tells them what gross profit they're likely to achieve, and the window of time they have to achieve it before holding costs, fluctuations in market values, and other factors may erode their potential return.

"The scores help us cure potential problems," says Duncan, who adds that these sessions allow managers to make adjustments to pricing and appraisal values to accommodate the needs of either the new or used vehicle department. His main focus, however, is making sure that he's not saddling fresh used inventory with added costs that could wipe out his gross profit potential.

Other dealers use the score as a key barometer on whether a trade-in vehicle should go into inventory or not. I know several dealers who immediately wholesale fresh trade-in units because the score shows the investment prospects are grim.

This approach may seem sacrilegious to most dealers and used vehicle managers, but it reveals a level of sophistication that today's used vehicle marketplace demands: if you know up-front that a vehicle doesn't make any sense from an investment perspective, why bother with it at all?

The score is really a forecast of how well a particular vehicle will perform as an investment opportunity for a given store. The score is derived from the same kinds of questions and data that a financial advisor like Tony Richards would consider when evaluating an investment opportunity:

- What's the market value or the right price for the investment (vehicle)? As you make an appraisal, the vAuto system pings the relevant pricing guides for your market area (NADA, Kelley Blue Book, etc.) and provides the market price. As your proposed appraisal amount veers up or down from the market value, the score changes. For example, if you decide you need to add $2,000 to a $10,000 car, the appraisal score for a given vehicle would be lower. The reasoning should be self-evident. By over-allowing on the appraisal, you're effectively hampering the vehicle's ability to perform as an investment because you've built in added acquisition costs up front. Similarly, if your appraisal is back of book, the score would be higher, reflecting the fact that you have a greater opportunity to yield your expectations for investment return.

- How much profit do you want to make on your vehicle investment? At most stores I work with, we ask this question to provide a benchmark by

which the vAuto system can evaluate the quality
of an appraisal and the effect the appraisal has
on achieving a store's gross profit expectations.
At most stores, an average $2,000-$2,500 gross
profit on used vehicles is a frequent target. So, if
you over-allow $2,000 on a trade-in, the vAuto
score is lower, reflecting the fact that you'll have
a harder time achieving your gross profit target.
The converse is also true: back of book deals earn
a higher score because your chances of meeting or
exceeding your gross profit target is greater.

- How long should you hold on to your investment
to achieve your return? Just as a financial advisor
asks an investor how long they're willing to wait
to achieve their return on investment, the vAuto
system poses the same question to dealers. In
many cases, dealers will offer a 45- or 60-day
window in which they hope to achieve their
return on investment.

The vAuto scoring system accounts for this time
horizon and factors in the appraisal amount,
average holding costs, depreciation and market
price changes to alert dealers of the timeframe
when they can expect to make the investment
return they seek. The system also accounts for a

store's past history at selling a particular make and model to forecast how long a vehicle may sit in inventory before it sells.

In most cases, the break-even point for used vehicles occurs well before the 45- or 60-day window.

Take the vehicle you may have appraised for $2,000 above its market value. Its score will reflect the fact that you've over-paid for the vehicle and that your chances of earning the expected $2,000-$2,500 gross profit have diminished. The system will also let dealers and used vehicle managers know when they need to take action on a vehicle to avoid or minimize a loss on their investment in a vehicle—whether it's 5, 10, 15, or 20 days, etc.

Table 6: The vAuto Appraisal Process

	Scenario 1	Scenario 2
What's the right price to pay ?	$10,000	$10,000
Your dealership's target gross profit	$2,500	$2,500
Average retail price of comparable vehicles within a 50 mile radius of your dealership	$11,000	$11,000
Your markup	$2,500	$1,000
Your retail price	$12,500	$11,000
Likelihood of selling your vehicle at your asking price	low	high

HOW A SCORE HELPS DEALERS AND USED VEHICLE MANAGERS

Dealers and used vehicle managers who use the vAuto scoring system say that it offers two key benefits:

1. **They know up front whether an appraisal or investment in a used vehicle makes sense from an investment perspective.** Dealers can punt on vehicles that are dogs right out of the gate. That's a far better approach than holding on to the vehicle and believing that it might sell.

2. **They have a better understanding of how well each appraiser is doing.** In addition to offering a score on the actual appraisal amount for a vehicle, the vAuto system also provides dealers and used vehicle managers with an overview or score of the performance of each person who handles an appraisal.

With the click of a mouse, a manager can tell who has a history of appraising vehicles too high or too low, or whether they're right on the money. The system gives a "look to book" report on each appraiser, which reveals some of the dynamics that too often go unwatched and unmanaged in most showrooms. In essence, you have a ready-made management tool that helps you spot the expert appraisers and those who require additional training.

For example, at a dealership in Colorado, the store's GM monitors appraiser performance. "I have a guy who takes in 60 percent of what he appraises, and they're all virtually right on the money," the GM says.

So what does the GM do with that information? He shows others, whose scores aren't as good, the process that enables the appraiser to manage customer expectations about trade-in values and achieve an appraisal that leaves both the dealership and customer satisfied. Hint: the GM says one of the appraiser's key tactics is spending time with customers and walking around a vehicle to understand its history. He also accompanies customers on appraisal test drives to let them see first-hand what issues may affect his appraisal offer.

SOME ADDITIONAL WORDS ABOUT INVESTMENT-MINDED VEHICLE ACQUISITIONS

The bulk of this chapter covers how investment principles can be a foundation for decisions dealers and used vehicle managers make in appraising and acquiring used vehicles through customer trades.

There are two additional points to be made about acquisitions.

First, using an investment-minded approach for used vehicle appraisals does not mean you cannot be aggressive about how you acquire vehicles. It is okay to step up and pay big money for a unit, provided your decision meets two conditions:

1. You have a good reason for doing it. It might be a big financing opportunity or you need to step up your new vehicle volume. Whatever the case, a decision to step up should be made with

the full knowledge and understanding that the additional money you pay has direct bearing on your store's investment position in the unit.

2. You have a plan for dealing with it. When an investment's troubled from the get-go, a financial advisor pays close attention to enhance the investment's chances of delivering a return or minimizing a loss. The same should be true for vehicles you step up to acquire. Your plan might be to wholesale the vehicle right away or set an aggressive price to move it quickly. Whatever the case, the old idea that you can retail your way out of the vehicle's troubled equity position is a mistake. The investment's troubled and your plan for managing this unit must treat it that way.

Second, most dealerships simply cannot source all of their used vehicles through trade-ins, so auctions are a necessary component of ensuring you have marketable breadth and depth in your inventory.

The vAuto system empowers used vehicle managers and buyers at auctions with the same type of score that they would use to guide an appraisal. The difference is that they need only input a prospective purchase price, or price range, on a given make and model to determine how well a vehicle will perform as an investment once they take it into inventory.

At stores that use the system, used vehicle managers will plug in the models and prospective price points they're willing to pay *before* they go to the auction. For them, the score is a way of hedging their risk that they might purchase a vehicle for the wrong price and saddle the used vehicle department with a future wholesale loss.

We all know that auctions can be a fun and exciting place to purchase vehicles. It's kind of like gambling ... though the managers are gambling with someone else's money. We also know that the coolest heads typically prevail when it comes to any form of gambling.

So who do you think is better prepared to win at an auction? The used vehicle manager who has a gut feel about what price he should pay for a vehicle or the manager who's got a score to accompany the purchase price and knows, with some degree of certainty, what he can afford to pay for a given vehicle to achieve his gross profit or return on investment expectations?

Injecting Honesty and Investment Smarts into Wholesale Dispositions

Some of you won't like what I'm about to say about the way most dealers and used vehicle managers handle the wholesaling of units in their used vehicle departments.

The fact is, most dealers and used vehicle managers are just going through the motions as they try to minimize wholesale losses and dispose of vehicles. If that wasn't the case, why is it the same story month after month? A used vehicle manager trots out an aged vehicle report, discusses plans for disposing of these vehicles through wholesale buyers and auctions and, if a store's lucky, the process nets only a minimal wholesale loss.

This scenario is, more than likely, just a shell game.

Don't believe me?

Try this exercise: take a look at the list of units your store has wholesaled to buyers or taken to auctions in each of the past three months. If your store is like most, many of the vehicles sat in your inventory for 45 to 60 days and, for all intents and purposes, were probably sold at or near the price you paid for them.

Take a deeper look and give me an honest answer to the following three questions:

1. How many of those units were in your inventory for just a few days?

2. How many of those units actually generated a wholesale profit when they were sold to a buyer or at auction?

3. How often did the sale of these vehicles make the difference in whether your used vehicle department generated a wholesale profit or loss for the month?

See where the shell game analogy comes from? The reality at most of the stores is that there are too many wholesale units that should have not gone to a wholesale buyer at all. In fact, these units—many of them fresh or relatively so—could likely have generated a decent return on investment as retail units.

But these vehicles weren't given a chance. To this, I would say, "Shame on all of us."

This shell game is the same one I played as a dealer. It's how you and I were both taught how to manage the used vehicle department. We grew up in the business thinking that we could always retail our way out of a problem.

But, as I've noted in previous chapters, we can no longer trust this axiom to work in our favor. So we let vehicles sit, holding out hope for a deal and then we've got an age problem!

The fix for all of this is an overhaul of the management practices that most dealers and used vehicle managers use to guide their decisions about when to wholesale a vehicle.

We need to face up to the practice of using wholesale dispositions to mask and make up for the mistakes used vehicle appraisers and managers made with other vehicles in our inventory. Let's be honest about what's going on: the decisions to wholesale the fresh units are really hedges against the losses created when an appraiser puts too much into a trade-in or a used vehicle manager fails to make adjustments, lot placement, appearance improvements, pricing changes, sales team spiffs, etc., when a vehicle starts to look like it's going to be a slow seller.

So it's these mistakes that occur early on in a vehicle's lifecycle that require attention and remediation. Other dealers have stood up to this problem and made changes. When they do, they start to realize that all their efforts to manage the age problem were really misdirected. I sometimes make the joke, which is all too true, that if you hire somebody to manage age, they've got a job for life.

AGE ISN'T THE PROBLEM, IT'S A SYMPTOM

If nothing else, this chapter should leave you with one key take-away: when a vehicle hits 45 or more days in inventory, it's really a sign that some part of your management of that vehicle's life cycle went awry. You've made a mistake—and it's best to be honest about the mistake, figure out why and do your best job to avoid a repeat.

Here are the common culprits for aging problems:

- **The initial appraisal.** An appraisal that's $2,000 more than book value, even though it helps close a new car sale, saddles the used unit with an additional $2,000 in acquisition costs and likely results in an asking price that's not realistic for today's price-informed used vehicle buyers. In many cases, this is a guarantee that a vehicle will grow long in the tooth. Some stores that own up to this practice charge the new vehicle department for whatever amount they stretched to make the deal. You don't need to go that far, but there's undoubtedly room for improvement in the way your people appraise vehicles.

  When a vehicle hits 45 or more days in inventory, it's really a sign that some part of your management of that vehicle's life cycle went awry. You've made a mistake—and it's best to be honest about the mistake, figure out why and do your best job to avoid a repeat.

- **Your pricing.** Most stores set the retail asking prices for their used vehicles based on how much they paid to acquire them. Therefore, if you made the decision to add $2,000 to an appraisal, you're basically asking your future retail buyer to pay extra for the profit you ceded to your new vehicle department, a deal your buyer had nothing to do with. You could argue that the over-appraisals that lead to higher retail asking prices are a cost of doing business—and that there's nothing wrong with trying to recoup your costs. I don't disagree.

But, unlike the past, we can no longer get away with this practice. Today's buyers are using the Internet and price is a primary motivator when they decide to call a dealership about a vehicle. If your pricing is not competitive, you won't get the call.

That's why the traditional pricing method is a recipe for profit and wholesale loss disasters.

- **Your merchandising.** I don't know any dealers or used vehicle managers who would consider it anything less than smart and wise to examine every unit in their used vehicle inventory every day and ask why it hasn't sold. But we all know this doesn't happen, except at really well-managed stores. The fact is, however, that in many stores this is more of a policy on paper than an actual practice. Consequently, the ability to make pricing and other adjustments at five, 10, 15 or 20 day intervals to make a vehicle more attractive to potential buyers just doesn't happen. We all know what comes next ... an age problem.

- **Your sales team.** Salespeople are notorious for taking the path of least resistance that will make them the most money. What happens when a salesperson knows that your store put too much money into a trade? I'll tell you: salespeople will immediately know that the unit's gross profit potential has diminished, as has their ability to maximize commission. Similarly, if a vehicle is getting old in your inventory, it carries a black mark. Salespeople understandably start to believe that something must not be right with the unit, otherwise it would have already been sold.

When you look at each of these individual culprits, it's no wonder many stores have an aging problem. The ironic thing is that, just like I did when I was a dealer, many dealers and used vehicle managers create and nurture their age problem every day.

Table 7: Common Causes for Aging Problems

Cause	Result
Poor initial appraisal	Saddles the used unit with additional acquisition costs and likely results in an asking price that's too high for today's price-informed buyers.
Poor pricing	Padding the appraisal means asking a future retail buyer to pay above market price because of profit that was already ceded to the new vehicle department.
Poor merchandising	Neglecting to make pricing and other adjustments at five-, 10-, 15- or 20-day intervals fails to make a vehicle more attractive to potential buyers.
Poor incentives for the sales team	Salespeople know when their store has put too much money into a trade and when the unit's gross profit potential has diminished. If their compensation is based on gross profit, they will not be motivated to sell low gross profit vehicles.

Using investment risk and return to guide wholesaling decisions

"I make decisions about what to wholesale based on their break-even point, or when I'll either make or lose money from an investment perspective," says a successful GM who's adopted an investment-minded approach to managing used vehicles. "I've talked to a lot of used vehicle managers and dealers and nobody I know in our business looks at it that way."

I was delighted to hear this comment recently. The fact is, I couldn't have said it better myself. Too few dealers and used vehicle managers use principles of investment management in their used vehicle operations, and nowhere is it more important than in making the decision about whether to keep or wholesale a vehicle.

In most cases, the decision to wholesale or retain a vehicle is made without anyone—not the used vehicle manager, not the GM and certainly not the dealer— really thinking about it like an astute financial advisor.

Let's start with the frequency by which wholesale decisions occur in dealerships. In most cases, it happens once a month. If you knew that your stockbroker or investment advisor was only looking at your portfolio once a month, do you think you'd be making as much money as you possibly could? If you're anything like me, I'd find someone who's more proactive with my money. When it comes to investments, you simply have to pay more attention than once a month.

The same is true with the investment dealers and used vehicle managers make in their used vehicle inventories. Someone *has* to pay attention to the inventory as an investment every day.

This daily review is even more critically important for used vehicle inventories than any other type of investment. Think about it: each day, the value of your investment in a used vehicle depreciates. I can't think of another type of investment that loses value every day.

That's why dealers and used vehicle managers need to ask themselves every day for every unit in their inventory, "can I still make a return or profit on my investment?"

They also need to ask: "If I sold today, what profit would I get?" and "What should I be doing differently with my price or positioning to improve our chances of selling the unit?"

Are you thinking that that's impossible to do? It is possible. Jerrod Musser does it. Tom Shirey does it. Gary Duncan does it. These guys are asking these questions every day, and they're seeing fewer wholesale losses and improved profits as a result.

THE INVESTMENT DATA YOU NEED IS RIGHT AT YOUR FINGERTIPS

I should clarify something: none of the dealers mentioned in this book sits down with the stock reports on each vehicle and sifts through them each day to find potentially troubled investments. They've turned to software and data to help them ask those critical investment-based questions and get the answers they need to manage their used vehicle investments profitably.

These dealers have instant access to the critical financial metrics they need at the moment they need it. For example, if you took in a 2005 Ford Explorer on a Monday for $10,000 and priced it at $14,000, the vAuto system would show that you can only achieve the $2,000 gross profit you want to make for the next 10 days. After that, due to depreciation, store history and market pricing shifts, the system would show that you may only expect to make $1,800 in gross after 10 days, and that you may even need to lower your asking price to get it.

If this dealer decides to retain a vehicle for retail, the vAuto system advises him on how depreciation and other costs affect his gross profit. He'll know exactly when it's time to readjust the price or spiff the unit to give it a better shot at selling. All along the way, he has his eye trained on his investment return. If the prospect of a solid gross profit gets too iffy, he'll punt and take what he can get, right then and there.

A GAME PLAN FOR ADDRESSING "CARS AT RISK"

Astute dealers use a lot of different approaches to have these "How's my investment in used vehicles doing?" discussions with used vehicle managers.

Make no mistake: as difficult as the conversation may be, the simple fact that you have the dialogue means you're in a far better position, from an investment standpoint, than dealers and used vehicle managers who rarely, if ever, talk about why a vehicle has or may become a risky investment.

Similar to the bullpen discussion that Gary Duncan uses for appraisals, I recommend that dealers and used vehicle managers conduct a "Cars at Risk" discussion at least weekly. The meeting should focus on the 10 vehicles in your used vehicle inventory that are most at risk from an investment standpoint. Keep in mind that the age, make and model of these vehicles doesn't matter; you may have a troubled vehicle, investment-wise, that's only been in your inventory for two or three days and appears to be the right car.

The key is that you'll be eyeing the investment break-
even point for each vehicle on the list. Or, put another
way, you'll be looking at those vehicles that either
have already, or will soon, start to cost you money.

A store's GM should facilitate the discussion, applying
just a handful of questions to each vehicle on the list.
There should be no finger-pointing. The purpose is to
look at your inventory through the raw, objective lens
of investment financial data. The questions:

- **Do you agree that we have a problem with this
  car?** This question functions as a gut-check and
  establishes common ground. A GM may look at
  the financial data and believe there's a problem.
  A used vehicle manager may know more. There
  could well be reasons that a particular vehicle is an
  investment risk that lay outside the raw financial
  data—a spate of lousy weather that depressed
  shoppers or an ad flight that didn't hit when it
  should. Those factors don't change the reality of
  the vehicle's risk of losing money, but they can
  provide context for a meaningful discussion on
  what to do, or not do, next.

- **What is the plan for disposition of the vehicle?**
  The question helps to pinpoint what managers
  think is the best course of attack, lowering the
  price, spiffing salespeople, moving it to another

store, etc., if you decide to retail the vehicle rather than wholesale it right away. If the decision is made to wholesale the vehicle, the GM and used vehicle manager should set a time and channel for this to occur.

- **Is the vehicle ready to go?** The question simply ensures that if you are going to retail the vehicle, it's definitely lot-ready. It's necessary, on occasion, for the GM and used vehicle manager to actually look at a vehicle to see if it's really lot-ready.

- **Is the vehicle priced correctly?** You can price yourself out of the buying market if you're asking too much to be competitive. There are lots of ways to get a read on where you stand: scan the Internet for pricing on similar vehicles, check newspaper ads, visit a competitor's store, review customer offers on the vehicle, and check prices on recent deals you've made with similar vehicles to gauge whether your asking price is sensible.

As these discussions occur, you may well decide to lower the asking price. It's okay to do this, even though it may generate less gross, if you know the margin is still better than what you'd get if you wholesaled the vehicle. Conversely, if you can't make those pricing changes, then it may well signal that it's time to wholesale the unit.

- **At what date, if we still have this vehicle, will we say that our plan didn't work?** Sometimes even the best strategies don't work. Asking this question is a way to say it's okay if Plan A doesn't work out. It also suggests that it's wise to have a workable Plan B in mind.

Be forewarned that these discussions do not come without some discomfort for used vehicle managers. After all, this discussion revisits decisions they have made and you're asking them to affirm whether their decisions are, in fact, in the best financial interest of the store.

Questions for a GM to ask to address "Cars at Risk"

1. Do you agree that we have a problem with this car?

2. How will we dispose of the vehicle?

3. Is the vehicle ready to go?

4. Is the vehicle priced correctly?

5. What date, if we still have this vehicle, will we say that our plan didn't work?

The key to making these meetings successful is a constructive tone. The goal is to give everyone the opportunity to take positive, profit-minded, corrective action to make sure any missteps aren't allowed to make things worse. In time, as both your GM and managers become more accustomed to asking these questions, there will be no surprises.

I've seen time and again at stores where a strategy like this is deployed, the risk of wholesale losses diminishes and the potential to turn more vehicles and do more volume increases.

THE HIDDEN COST OF DOING NOTHING

Once you deploy a more investment-minded approach to managing the dispositions of your used vehicle inventory, you correct another problem that often goes undetected and unnoticed in most dealers' used vehicle departments: the cost of waiting for a car to sell.

What I mean by this is fairly simple: for every vehicle that's in your used vehicle inventory, there are others that could easily take its place. If you've placed your bet on a vehicle that doesn't appear likely to generate the financial return you need, and you don't have the mechanisms to identify and dispose of the mistake before it reaches 30, 45 or

60 days, you've effectively killed any opportunity to offer another vehicle that will perform better than the one you've got.

In other words, you are reducing the possibility of delivering a better return on your investment—just because you've chosen not to pay attention to existing problems in your inventory.

Neither scenario is acceptable. In today's market, it's necessary to make sure that every vehicle in your inventory represents the best investment possible. If your approach is anything less than that, your used vehicle department will never be as competitive as those dealerships that live and breathe this kind of investment-minded disposition discipline or as profitable as it could be.

Today's used vehicle marketplace requires more skill and sophistication when it comes to pricing and establishing gross profit targets than simply marking up a unit (pack and all) and hoping that you might "get lucky" on a car.

VIEWING RECONDITIONING AS AN INVESTMENT, NOT AS AN EXPENSE

No one argues that it makes good sense to put a used vehicle into the best condition possible to make it attractive to potential buyers. Reconditioning is a necessary part of any successful used vehicle department.

But here's where current industry practices turn this rather simple notion on its head: most dealers and used vehicle managers view reconditioning as a kind of necessary evil, an expense they'd rather live without.

Try taking an investment-minded mentality to reconditioning. Rather than viewing reconditioning as an expense, dealers and used vehicle managers should think of it as an investment opportunity—a method by which you can add value to your original investment in a vehicle.

And, like any investment, dealers and used vehicle managers should also apply principles of astute investment management to every reconditioning decision they make. The reality is that not every so-called right vehicle deserves to get reconditioned and retailed.

Take a unit you paid up to acquire. Let's say you paid $1,000 more for a vehicle than its book value. Does it make sense to add an additional $600 to $800 in reconditioning costs, and potentially create a situation where this vehicle is $1,600 under water before you've even had a chance to sell it?

The answer, of course, is that it may be a wise investment decision, or it may not. But in far too many cases, dealers and used vehicle managers aren't even asking those questions before they make a decision to recondition vehicles.

I've seen it time and again: a used vehicle manager has a stack of ROs for reconditioning that require approval. Invariably, the used vehicle manager just thumbs the stack and signs every one of them. The signed ROs then go back to service and no one has really assessed whether these additional costs make sense from an investment perspective.

Used vehicle managers absolutely take notice when a reconditioning expense is extraordinary—say a vehicle needs transmission work or has a chronic idling problem. But these are largely an exception to the rote, sign-it-and-move-on reflex that most used vehicle managers apply to their reconditioning decisions. It's as if the initial $600 or more in reconditioning expense is throw-away money.

I would assert that such reflexive, non-investment minded decisions about reconditioning are one, if not the, chief reason why many vehicles end up creating wholesale losses. In simple terms, the absence of investment-minded management in this phase of a vehicle's life cycle at a dealership often amounts to throwing good money after bad.

It doesn't have to be this way. There are two key takeaways on this topic:

1. Reconditioning is an investment, not an expense.

2. You should make reconditioning decisions with a full awareness of the effect these decisions will have on the value of the investment you've made in a vehicle and its potential return.

Applying an investment perspective to reconditioning

Flash back to that used vehicle manager with the stack of reconditioning ROs that require approval. His marching orders are fairly straightforward: unless a unit's recon costs falls outside the store's benchmark of $600 or $800, the recon work will get instant approval.

From a surface perspective, one could argue that this used vehicle manager is applying an investment perspective: he's got a threshold at which he'll take a deeper look to determine if the added costs for reconditioning make sense for a given vehicle. There's at least some recognition that if you overspend on reconditioning, you'll sink a vehicle's chances to deliver a return on investment when it's sold.

But here's the problem: not every vehicle that falls within the reconditioning benchmark actually deserves the additional dollars. That's because the used vehicle manager isn't asking the two all-important questions that account for the investment prospects of each vehicle in his inventory: does this unit actually deserve to get reconditioned? What effect will the additional reconditioning costs have on the ability of this vehicle to generate a respectable return on investment?

The fact is, some vehicles, including those we deem to be the right vehicles, may not deserve the additional investment, especially those units that were purchased for too much money in the first place. In those cases, the additional dollars spent on reconditioning are only adding weight to the vehicle's ability to generate a decent return on investment. Put another way, you're taking on more risk (in the form of added costs) that can impede your investment's return potential.

In many stores I visit, dealers and used vehicle managers are not asking whether reconditioning is worth it from an investment perspective, they're just green-lighting every recon job, unless there's a serious problem that requires more service work and cost than what they customarily allow.

It's not difficult to discern the reasons for this reflexive style of operation: every one of the reconditioning decisions relates to a fresh car and we all know that fresh cars are likely to sell better and faster and produce more gross profit than older vehicles. What's more, when you have dealers and used vehicle managers who cling to the idea that the right buyer will come along, there's no reason to think critically about the effect the additional reconditioning costs will have on a unit's prospects for generating a respectable return on investment.

> *When your used vehicle manager simply okays the majority of reconditioning work, there's no recognition of whether the added costs have essentially sunk a vehicle's potential to make a return on investment.*

But this approach to reconditioning is problematic from an investment perspective. The additional reconditioning costs can make an already investment-troubled vehicle a bigger problem.

Here's what I mean: when your used vehicle manager simply okays the majority of reconditioning work, there's no recognition of whether the added costs have essentially sunk a vehicle's potential to make a return on investment.

Take a unit that you paid up to acquire in a trade-in or at an auction. If you paid $10,000 to acquire a vehicle that's only worth $9,000, you've already saddled the unit with an additional $1,000 in costs. When you add in the $600 for reconditioning work, you now have an additional $1,600 in costs that you need to recover.

At most stores, the solution for this problem is simply marking up the vehicle's asking price to account for the additional $1,600 in costs.

In past years, this was largely okay. We all believed the right buyer would come along and pay our asking price, and they often did. But, as we've discussed in earlier chapters, today's market is no longer as forgiving.

In some ways, the practice of adding reconditioning costs into your pricing effectively functions as a pack. When you base your retail pricing on your costs, arbitrary or not, you may well be making your vehicles less competitive in a marketplace that requires a greater degree of on-target pricing to attract price sensitive buyers.

INTELLIGENT RECONDITIONING REQUIRES AWARENESS

So how do you properly recondition vehicles and price them to attract buyers and remain mindful of each unit's prospects as a profit-generating investment?

The vAuto system offers one pathway. It recognizes the role that reconditioning plays in helping or hurting a used vehicle's potential as an investment.

For example, the system would show that a vehicle you purchased for $10,000 and priced for $12,000 is likely to generate $2,000 of gross profit. If you add $500 in reconditioning costs, the system shows that your likely gross profit will be $1,500 and offers a lower score on the vehicle to reflect its diminished potential to generate a return on investment.

You can also use the system to adjust retail asking prices to essentially vector your way to determining the threshold at which additional reconditioning costs still enable you to make a respectable return on your investment.

Taken together, these two features enable you to determine whether a vehicle deserves to get reconditioned and how much you can afford to spend on reconditioning to achieve your desired return on investment. Furthermore, it ensures that your vehicle is competitive from a pricing standpoint.

This approach makes a whole lot more financial sense than the way most dealers and used vehicle managers handle reconditioning and pricing today.

Dealers and used vehicle managers who apply an investment perspective to their reconditioning decisions actually find that they spend less on reconditioning because they're more selective about the vehicles that get reconditioned and the extent of the work they'll do to bring a vehicle up to their standards for lot-readiness. I'm not suggesting these dealers are cutting corners, because they're not.

These dealers and used vehicle managers are buying and pricing vehicles smarter. They know up front that if they plan to retail a vehicle, and spend $600-$800 to get it ready for sale, they'd better do their best to acquire the vehicle at the lowest price possible to keep their investment costs to a minimum.

When it comes to pricing, these dealers and used vehicle managers also recognize that any additional costs for reconditioning have a direct impact on the return they can expect to get. They aren't naively marking up their asking prices to recoup their costs; they're setting prices that are realistic and accepting the reality that additional costs for reconditioning may well translate to a smaller gross profit.

Dealers and used vehicle managers who make it a practice to apply investment-based management principles to their reconditioning efforts are buying vehicles smarter and marking them up more realistically than those who stick with the tried and true practice of pricing vehicles based on their ACV, irrespective of what the market will bear.

For dealers and used vehicle managers who understand and apply investment-based management principles, the benefits are profound. They actually pay less in reconditioning expenses and move vehicles more efficiently and profitably than those who do not deploy investment-minded discipline.

For dealers and used vehicle managers who understand and apply investment-based management principles, the benefits are profound. They actually pay less in reconditioning expenses and move a greater number of vehicles more efficiently and profitably than those who do not deploy investment-minded discipline in their used vehicle operations.

THE CORROSIVE EFFECTS OF AN "EXPENSE" MENTALITY

We can't leave the topic of reconditioning without addressing one of the chief bugaboos that plagues many dealerships' used vehicle departments: reconditioning gets a low priority in service and vehicles often sit for days in service departments awaiting this necessary work.

This is a problem because, as we've established in earlier chapters, time is not your friend in the used vehicle business. Every additional day a vehicle sits in your inventory unready for sale is another day's worth of holding costs and lost opportunity to garner your expected return on your investment in the vehicle.

So why is this still an issue nearly 80 years later? It goes back to the long-held idea, which today's market forces have eroded, that time will eventually produce a buyer who will pay our asking price. Therefore, an extra day or two lost while a vehicle awaits reconditioning, regardless of the cost this delay creates, is not really a big deal.

But, when you regard each used vehicle as an investment, it is a big deal. That's why some dealerships actually set firm turnaround times and penalize the department that causes the delays.

IT'S ALL ABOUT TURN AND VELOCITY

Dealer John Schenden of Pro Chrysler Jeep in Denver told me that today's used vehicle business requires constant attention and a focus on moving vehicles in and out of your inventory quickly. "It's all about turn and velocity," he says.

In his view and mine, any unnecessary delays in reconditioning vehicles represent the costs of lost opportunities, on top of the added costs of holding a vehicle for a few additional days. Think of it this way: in essence, you're parking your investment in a non-interest-bearing account while you decide what to do with it. Would you find it acceptable if your investment advisor took the same approach to your personal portfolio?

Speaking for myself, I'd want to charge that advisor for the lost time and interest I might have earned had he been more diligent and proactive with my money. The same is true for dealerships. Some dealers have implemented penalties for reconditioning delays to be paid by the service department or whomever's responsible.

I can't tell you what your optimal reconditioning time should be. Some stores do it in two or three days. Some do it in four or five. The key point is that you should have a target turnaround time and a process you follow diligently with every vehicle to do your best to meet the target and generate the maximum return possible for your investment in a used vehicle.

Gary Duncan uses his pay plans to create a sense of urgency with reconditioning. It starts by counting a vehicle as part of his inventory the moment it gets purchased, whether it's through a trade-in or auction sale. Then, his managers make a bonus based on keeping every unit in their inventories at or below 30 days. If they let a vehicle go longer, the monthly bonus of $500 goes unpaid.

It's difficult to get policies like these implemented. After all, the used vehicle department isn't going anywhere, and service managers and technicians know this. Even so, there's no reason why any dealer's used vehicle department should be held hostage to a service department that chooses not to make reconditioning a greater priority.

Any delay from the point of acquisition to the day a vehicle is ready for retail hurts your investment and its potential to deliver a return.

Remember: any delay from the point of acquisition to the day a vehicle is ready for retail hurts your investment and its potential to deliver a return.

How Investment-Minded Management Improves Desking

Virtually every customer who walks into General Sales Manager Ellen Schmidt's office at Morrie's Mazda in Minneapolis wants a better price on the vehicle they're planning to purchase than what the store is offering.

"They'll always ask, 'how much cheaper will you go?'" Schmidt says. She understands the dynamic: customers are looking for a deal that they can feel good about. Plus, there's another dynamic at work, too. Customers these days have done their homework and, right or wrong, they have a price in mind for what they think a particular vehicle is worth.

In previous years, Schmidt had little choice but to do the same thing nearly every desking manager in a franchised dealership would do. She'd insist that the store's price was the best the store could offer and that it was the best deal on the vehicle the customer was likely to find.

The problem: even though Schmidt may have believed what she was telling her customer, she could tell that many customers didn't really swallow the juice. Their doubt showed in their eyes, their body language and, on occasion, the speed with which they left her office.

"The worst thing that can happen is the customer feels like they got a bad deal," Schmidt says. "Most customers just want to know or affirm that they're getting a fair deal."

These days, however, few customers leave Schmidt's office thinking they got a raw deal. In fact, Schmidt says it's a rare day when she can't come to terms with a customer and prove that the price she's offering is, in fact, the best deal on the market for her customer.

"In the past, I couldn't gather enough research to show that our prices are aggressive and competitive," says Schmidt, who notes that Morrie's is a store that markets itself as a low-price leader. "Now, I have everything I need at my fingertips to show the market to the customer. It's a super-huge advantage for me."

Schmidt gains her market knowledge and competitive advantage by using the vAuto system as a desking tool. With the click of her mouse, she can show a customer a vehicle's competitive positioning in her market area and, if necessary, prove to the customer why her vehicle is a better buy than another similar unit that may be priced for less.

"This tool makes us a whole lot more believable than we could have been in the past," she says. "Customers actually know what I'm saying is true."

Schmidt says her closing ratio on desking deals is higher than it's ever been and, because she's able to demonstrate why the store's price is right for a customer, the store's far more consistent about maintaining the gross profit it needs in every deal.

Schmidt says the tool also gives her another advantage. "It helps me keep the customers honest," she says. Sometimes they're just fishing for a deal they know is unrealistic. And, when she shows them how far off their price is compared to other competitive listings, there's often a wry smile and an acknowledgement from the customer that he or she was just testing to see if Schmidt would bite on another price.

The data and transparency that Schmidt uses in her office every day is a far cry from the way desking is handled and managed at most stores today.

By and large, the majority of desking decisions are subjective calls that often have nothing to do with the two central questions any desking manager should be asking: is the price on this deal, at this moment, a good return on investment for our store? And is the price on this deal, at this moment, one that will leave my customer with a favorable impression?

Too often desking managers aren't asking these important questions, which means they're taking or rejecting deals for the wrong reasons. They may say yes to a deal because they need to move metal and meet a sales quota. They may say no because they believe today's offer may not be as good as one they'll get tomorrow, or maybe even next week.

Things are a whole lot different at Morrie's Mazda. There, Schmidt can tell you, at the moment a deal hits her desk, whether the store might be letting a car go for too little, or whether it's best to take today's short deal because it's not likely she will get a better offer.

Schmidt knows this because she checks virtually all factors that are in play at the time of a desking decision—the price the store paid for the vehicle, its depreciation and reconditioning costs, its likelihood to sell in the future, the competitiveness of the customer's offer or counter-offer and, of course, what return on investment the deal will generate for the store if she ultimately decides to do the deal.

How investment-based data makes desking more effective

Let's play out a hypothetical to see how investment-based data, when combined and analyzed to guide a desking decision, creates a powerful, profit-making tool for your store.

Assume you have a 2005 Trailblazer that has been in your store's used vehicle inventory for only three days. A customer has just made an offer that would yield a $200 gross profit. The desk manager, like most at sales desks, would likely have an immediate reaction: we do a good job with Trailblazers and this vehicle's very fresh. Wouldn't it be worthwhile to pass on this one and see if we can get a better deal?

Most desk managers would pass on the deal. The car's simply too fresh and, given the tradition of used vehicle managers and dealers to hold out for the highest-grossing retail deal, the $200 shortie seems almost foolish to accept.

But contrast this scenario with the same vehicle and offer—only this time let's bring in the process that Schmidt uses at Morrie's Mazda. Before saying yes or no to the deal, she will examine several indicators to drill into the investment status of the vehicle and decide what to do:

- **The ROI on the vehicle.** This is the initial, and most important, consideration. Schmidt will look first at how the store acquired the vehicle. Was it on the money? Did the store pay up to get it? Was it a solid, "back of book" deal?

   For our hypothetical, let's assume the store paid up $1,000 too much to acquire the Trailblazer on trade. Schmidt can see that the $1,000 over-appraisal has diminished the vehicle's return on investment potential. Instead of getting the average $1,500 the store typically gets for Trailblazers, she knows its gross profit or ROI potential is really only $500.

   Schmidt may look at the $200 offer and pass. The reason: if they wait and sell the vehicle fast enough, the store may see its full $500 potential return.

At this point, Schmidt and the typical desk manager could end up in the same place: passing on the deal.

But Schmidt won't take the pass until she has done evaluating a few other factors to determine how the deal stacks up as an investment. They include:

- **A review of whether the offer's competitive.** Given Morrie's pricing strategy, Schmidt is generally confident that the deals she offers are competitive—but she still takes a look at the marketplace just to be sure. She wants to know how the deal on the Trailblazer stacks up to the competition.

- **The store's past history selling Trailblazers.** Schmidt may find that the store typically sells Trailblazers after an average of 30 days in inventory. She now faces the question: can I afford to wait for a $500 gross profit deal or should I take the $200 deal today?

- **The effect of holding costs on investment return.** Given it takes an average of 30 days to sell Trailblazers, Schmidt could rationalize that it might take another 27 days (30 days minus the three days the Trailblazer's been in inventory) to retail the unit. She'd also see, first-hand, that the cost to keep the vehicle for 27 days could run $675 (assuming an average of $25/day to keep the vehicle in inventory).

See how the knee-jerk reaction to passing on the $200 short deal might be a mistake? If Schmidt chose to pass on the deal, she'd know the vehicle must be sold within 12 days—the point at which additional holding costs (12 days x $25/day=$300) whittles the potential $500 gross profit down to $200.

I can't tell you exactly what Schmidt would do in this situation. But I'd bet good money that she'd take the $200 deal today and move on. Her thinking might well go something like this: why fight to keep an additional $300 that may or may not come about in the next 12 days? Wouldn't I be better off moving this unit today and replacing it with something that will deliver more gross profit potential?

Table 8: A hypothetical example of how investment-based data makes desking more effective

	2005 Trailblazer
Days in dealer's inventory	3
Over-appraisal acquisition cost	$1,000
Gross profit on first customer offer	$200
Average historical profit on Trailblazers for this dealer	$1,500
ROI potential on this unit	$500
Average historical days it takes dealer to sell a Trailblazer	30
Estimated cost of holding unit an additional 27 days	$675
Days dealer has to sell this unit before reducing potential gross profit from $500 to $200, the amount of the first customer offer	12

The reality is that too few desking managers apply this kind of investment-based thinking to their daily decision-making. Most would pass on the $200 deal, and probably wind up with an aging unit. I understand why this happens. It's the old "hey, this is a fresh car and we can do better" mentality at work.

Unfortunately this type of thinking no longer works in today's more competitive and volatile used vehicle marketplace. Desking deals in today's market requires an investment-based mindset to make good decisions. As one dealer notes, good desking decisions are those that generate a maximum profit for the dealership and a satisfying experience for the customer.

You may be thinking, "Okay, you've given us an example that only serves to prove your point. What if we'd acquired the vehicle on the money and our managers and salespeople are savvy enough as prospectors and negotiators that we could turn that $200 offer into a $1,800 gross profit by waiting for another buyer?"

If that's the case, I'd tip my hat to you and say go for it. But I'd also suggest that you use caution. Just because you buy a vehicle on the money doesn't mean that you'll ever see the buyer who will give you the $1,800 gross profit deal you want, especially if your pricing is out of line.

Bringing additional, investment-minded data into desking decisions can only make your desking managers better at their jobs and more profitable for your dealerships and used vehicle departments. Unfortunately, at most dealership sales desks, this kind of thinking and use of investment-focused data about vehicles is virtually non-existent.

An honest look at today's desking shortfalls

When is the last time you did a "look at the ones that got away" analysis of your desking decisions?

Take a look at the units you wholesaled last month. How many offers on the vehicles did you reject before the unit became a wholesale problem? These are the deals that you probably should have taken, given the ultimate fate of the vehicle, but for some reason or another, you didn't.

There's a converse analysis that is also handy. Those are the ones that might have seemed like gross-profit winners and generated high-fives at the sales desk. But then somebody actually paid attention to the wholesale market value and what effect our buying the unit back of book had on the $2,000 gross profit deal we thought we had made. Oops. It turns out that the deal was a lot shorter than you thought.

Investment-minded desking decisions will reduce, if not eliminate, these kinds of scenarios from happening at your store. We can all agree that smarter desking decisions can be a key contributor to retaining gross profits and avoiding wholesale losses.

The disciplined use of investment-focused data also prevents desk managers from making decisions that are based on far more subjective considerations rather than the financial ones they should be heeding:

- **Pressure to move metal.** If a dealer or GM has just implored the desk to close more deals, it will always raise the pressure to take deals that may not be the best from an investment perspective for the store. In our hypothetical example above, taking the $200 deal would actually work out just fine. But, as we all know, that's just a stroke of luck rather than a smart decision, if the manager's just saying yes to deals to keep the dealer or GM from blowing a gasket because the sales volume's lagging behind a monthly goal.

- **Influence of pay plans.** Let's go back to our '05 Trailblazer and the $200 offer. I've already demonstrated why most desk managers would likely take a pass, the fresh car syndrome and the lure of a potentially bigger gross profit, coming from some future buyer, is just too strong.

Let's be honest: how much of that manager's decision to take or pass on the deal relates to the effect that decision will have on his or her paycheck? There's no way of knowing for sure, but I'd venture that it's a chief contributor to the judgment call.

What's more, if it turns out that the decision's a bad one from an investment perspective, the manager's paycheck most likely won't be affected. In most stores, the pay plans reward managers for decisions they make today and don't hold them accountable for the negative effect today's decision has on the store's investment in a vehicle in 30, 45 or 60 days.

The process of desking deals is simply too important to be left up to managers who are working with little more than gut-level guesses and hunches about whether taking or passing on a deal is a financially sound decision for the store.

The use of investment-minded data—the same stuff that Schmidt deploys every day on every deal that hits her desk—is essential to ensuring that your desking process is consistently focused on generating a return on investment for your store.

"I'd never go back to the old way of doing it," Schmidt says. "I've been enlightened and I am a believer in what this data can do for us."

Future Success Takes More Than Investment- Minded Management

Throughout this book, I've shared examples of dealers who've begun improving their inventory turn rates, sales volumes and gross profits by applying a more sophisticated, investment-minded strategy to their used vehicle departments.

But despite those successes, even those dealers recognize that the long-term success and viability of their used vehicle business requires more than applying an investment mindset to the acquisition, reconditioning, pricing, desking and disposition of vehicles. These dealers recognize such a solid investment-based foundation is but a mere foothold on the hill to success.

There is absolutely no question that fundamental selling techniques and merchandising skills are an essential and critical part of the used vehicle business for dealers. All the investment-minded management in the world won't help if your lot looks bad or your salespeople are excessively pushy or rude.

One of the nation's best traditional used vehicle GMs is Joe Ferezy of Galpin Motors in Los Angeles. Whenever I'm in town, I meet with Ferezy. It's usually at 6 a.m., after he's been on the job at least an hour—and there's a fair amount of strong coffee consumed.

Ferezy puts it this way, "Customers need to feel comfortable. Your place needs to be organized, inviting and cozy."

That's the attitude Ferezy brings to his job, and his people, every day. He even gets his lot vacuumed every day.

I share Ferezy's meticulous approach to managing used vehicle operations to underscore the point that traditional-minded merchandising and retailing skills remain an essential part of our business. Applying investment-minded management principles to your operation won't matter if you don't present them and, as Ferezy says, make your customers feel comfortable.

In my travels, I've run across sales practices and approaches at several stores—both from those that have adopted our software and those who haven't. I've seen several best-in-class ideas that would benefit any dealer or used vehicle manager. I share them here as an indication of the customer-focused attention more dealers and used vehicle managers are bringing into the business and, in some ways, as a warning for dealers who haven't yet recognized that many of the traditional approaches to managing a used vehicle department have become outmoded.

PROVIDING PEACE OF MIND *BEFORE* AND *AFTER* A PURCHASE

About 40 years ago, my father was a Buick dealer in Gary, Indiana. He offered customers something that was unheard of back then—he called it the Pollak Peace of Mind. His message to customers was a simple one: if you bought something from us and didn't like it, you could bring it back within 48 hours and get your money back. No questions asked.

For my father, this was more than a marketing tactic. He truly believed in treating customers right because he took a long view of the business. If you treat them right today, they'll come back again tomorrow.

As I scan today's used vehicle marketplace, I realize my father was on to something profound. Beyond just delivering top-notch customer satisfaction, he shouted that message from rooftops with a compelling and unique branding campaign that helped his store stand out from the competition.

As I talk with dealers and used vehicle managers about how they are differentiating their used vehicle departments from competitors', the phrase "peace of mind" keeps coming up. In fact, some dealers believe the competition in today's marketplace requires this type of branding message.

Gary Duncan has seen the rise of CarMax, the growth in private owner sales of used vehicles on eBay and other online sites and an increase in the volumes independent lots log each month in his region. He's taken all this, studied it, looked in the mirror and come to the following conclusion: there's something wrong with the way we have been doing this business for years.

In some ways, it's all a head-scratcher for Duncan. Why wouldn't a customer want to come to a dealership, where the need for a solid reputation and good customer service is necessary?

"Customers must really not like dealers all that much," Duncan concludes.

With that thought in mind, Duncan's taking several steps to change consumer perceptions and turn customers into what a popular business writer has dubbed "raving fans."

"CarMax has taught us something," Duncan says. "It's not all about the price. It's about the trust and confidence customers feel about your store. You don't have to be the cheapest if you're able to give peace of mind."

Duncan's not alone in his thinking. "We, as dealers, used to be first in line with customers. Now we're third in line behind eBay, CarMax and other non-dealer outlets," notes another dealer.

So what are these dealers doing? They're offering programs and policies that help brand their used vehicle operations as places customers can trust. The end-game is clear, just like it was for my father: if customers leave you feeling like they got a good deal and you're trustworthy, chances are they'll keep coming back.

Here's a glimpse at some approaches dealers like Duncan and others are taking to regain the trust and confidence of customers and sell them more used vehicles.

- **Guaranteed buy-backs.** More dealers are effectively taking this page from CarMax's playbook, offering three, five or seven-day buy-back guarantees. If you're not happy, you can come back and find the vehicle that's right for you. "Trust is a huge thing with our customers," says one dealer who firmly believes his buy-back program sets his store apart from competitors.

- **Warranty protection.** Ken Garff believes his company's "Mile after Mile" warranty program is one of the keys to the dealer group's ongoing growth in its used vehicle business and its rock-solid reputation with customers in its communities. And here's the kicker: customers get end-to-end coverage when they purchase vehicles, provided they come back to Garff stores for regular service and maintenance. It's a win-win.

Garff takes this interest in customer peace
of mind a step further. If customers purchase
a vehicle from Garff and maintain it at the
dealer group's stores, the company adds a $500
guaranteed trade-in boost, based on Kelley
Blue Book values. "Ultimately, if a car's been
maintained the way it should be, you'd pay $500
more for it," he says.

Ferezy has been offering a 6,000-mile, six-month
warranty on Galpin-certified vehicles for years.

- **Free vehicle history reports.** In the past few years,
this has become the norm, thanks to CarMax
making it a standard at its stores. Some dealers
don't provide the reports, either online or on
their lots, and it's just one more reason why a
customer may not want to shop your inventory
to find a vehicle.

- **More real-life pricing on dealership web sites.**
AutoTrader.com's Perry says that dealers still make
the mistake of believing that they need to build a
large gross profit into the asking prices they post
on their web sites.

As I shared in earlier chapters, that's a sure-fire
recipe for eliminating your store and used vehicle
inventory from the shopping lists of today's price-

conscious, Internet-enabled buyers. They know what a vehicle's worth and some may well be insulted when they see you asking a price with a $3,000 to $5,000 mark-up.

This isn't to say that rock-bottom pricing is the end-all for today's buyers. As Perry says, today's Internet shoppers are not as price sensitive as most dealers think. But you have to be *competitive* and then you need to provide them with a buying process that engenders trust and confidence to win their business.

> *Tom Shirey puts it this way, "Consumer trust allows you to not need to be the lowest price. But it's a whole package of perception that gives a dealer that advantage."*

Tom Shirey puts it this way, "Consumer trust allows you to not need to be the lowest price. But it's a whole package of perception that gives a dealer that advantage."

On Shirey's web site, he seeks to build trust by offering realistic prices and alerting customers to other dealers' tricks. His site notes that all of his prices *include* the cost of vehicle certification, a response to other dealers being less than candid about their online vehicle pricing.

Those are just a few of the best practices that dealers are undertaking to give their used vehicle departments a better shot at making deals with today's customers.

Table 9: How Dealerships Add Value beyond Price

Service	Value Add
Guaranteed buy backs	Builds trust, shows dealer is selling a quality product.
Warranty protection	Double win. Customers get end-to-end coverage when they purchase vehicle; dealer has a service customer for the lifetime of the vehicle.
Free vehicle history reports.	Builds trust; shows dealer has nothing to hide.
Realistic pricing on dealership web site	Builds trust. Acknowledges price-savvy buyers.

My question to you is this: what are you doing to make customers' peace of mind part of the culture at your store? I ask because it's become apparent that this emphasis is paying dividends, on top of smart, investment-minded management, in the form of repeat customers and referrals at stores that take this customer peace of mind seriously.

DALE'S CRYSTAL BALL: IS ONE-PRICE SELLING PART OF THE FUTURE?

As I was thinking about how to end this book, I had an idea: showcase a clear, shining example of what the power of investment-minded management can do for a used vehicle department and a dealership where investment-minded management practices may well be its sole salvation, particularly given the challenges of the current market environment.

With that in mind, I started to eliminate some dealership contenders. Stores in the Southwest or in California wouldn't work. Many of those markets are growing in terms of their populations and local economies. It would be easy for any reader to look at those examples and dismiss them as the obvious byproduct of being in the right market at the right time.

Similarly, dealers with desirable import franchises would also be suspect. We all know how a strong new vehicle franchise can be a sure-fire ticket to profitable used vehicle operations. These dealers have the innate benefit of a steady supply of fresh trades and financing flexibility that dealers with more troubled franchises can only hope to see.

This process of elimination led me to the door of Town Motors in Exton, Pennsylvania. Dealer Len Freed and his nephew, Maury, could easily have a *troubled* dealership and used vehicle department.

First, they are Chrysler dealers. As of this writing, the franchise is troubled. Sales are slow. The trade press is rife with stories of dealers bowing to factory pressures to take on additional new vehicle inventory because it is not selling fast enough.

Second, the Freeds work in a brutal marketplace. Any dealer who's knowledgeable about East Coast markets knows that, for car dealers, the City of Brotherly Love is anything but that. In fact, the metropolitan Philadelphia market may well be one of the most over-dealered and price-competitive regions in the country.

Despite all this, though, the Freeds and their used vehicle manager have set up a successful used vehicle operation. In fact, it may be one of the best in the business. It's lean, efficient and consistently profitable.

I looked up some of Town Motors' operational benchmarks to verify my hunch that the Freed's operation, fueled by an investment-minded management strategy, is a profit-making powerhouse.

For starters, the Freeds keep a tight control on their inventory. On average, they hold about $1.1 million worth of used vehicles. Their strategy turns on the concept of velocity. The Freeds know that if you source vehicles correctly, price them right and offer customers a compelling reason beyond just price to buy from their store, they will have a steady stream of floor traffic and willing buyers.

The inventory turn rate at Town Motors confirms this. The Freeds are able to turn the store's inventory 17 times a year. On top of that, the store's gross profits are beating national averages for used vehicles and its net profits are even more stellar, thanks to operational efficiencies—less advertising and personnel costs, to name two—that the Freeds and manager David Simches have been able to achieve.

The story behind the Freed's impressive results doesn't just come from their embrace of investment, or equity-minded, management principles. They also believe in one-price selling—an approach to retailing vehicles that, increasingly, I think will become the wave of the future.

For some of you, the mere mention of one-price selling may cause heartburn. But, as I've thought about how the used vehicle marketplace, the Internet and consumer preferences will evolve in the coming years, I'm increasingly confident in saying that one-price selling may well be how we all retail our vehicles in the next decade.

Remember the point I made earlier about how used vehicles have become commodities and, as a result, the prospect of high-dollar gross profits are an all-too-rare occurrence? This trend is not going away. In fact, it will become more pervasive as Internet access becomes more ubiquitous and more consumers have the ability to shop dealers more pointedly and precisely than they've done before.

In turn, this creates a challenge for dealers and their used vehicle managers. Many still only pay attention to two key metrics, their volume and average gross profit, as they manage their used vehicle operations. This thinking is a crude way to manage your potential for success in today's marketplace.

Sharp dealers like the Freeds have embraced this change. They recognize the business isn't about large, average gross profits anymore. Instead, they discipline themselves to become more efficient and price-competitive in how they manage their used vehicle operations. They've studied the trends and the successes of retailers like CarMax and Wal-Mart, and have applied some of the same astute inventory and pricing strategies that have made both of those companies highly successful.

For the Freeds, the one-price selling environment is their answer to these changing market dynamics. So far, it's proven successful and it has made a believer out of me. One-price selling, due to its keen focus on investment-minded management principles and processes, may well be the only way for dealers to take control of a more challenging and changed marketplace and continue to be profitable.

PRICE IT RIGHT AND THEY WILL COME

We all know the age-old industry axiom that if we buy a car right, it's already half-sold. Similarly, we all also know the saying that "your profit's made on the buy" of a used vehicle.

Most dealers understand the ever-important need to buy a vehicle right. The problem, as I've indicated in earlier chapters, is often that dealers are less astute about how they price their vehicles. Most dealers aren't using their own marketplaces as a pricing guide. They are setting retail asking prices based on how much they have invested in a vehicle or on the amount for which they own it.

At one-price stores, the exact opposite is true.

One-price operations are far more astute about their respective marketplaces than most traditional dealers. They have to be, because they know that a competitive price is one of the most important considerations for customers shopping for used vehicles. Today's customers know how to shop for vehicles online and if they find your price is out of line, they won't even bother sending you an e-mail or giving you a call.

It never ceases to amaze me when I meet with dealers who compete with a one-price store or a retailing operation like CarMax. These dealers scratch their heads and wonder how these competitors can even stay in business when they're often retailing vehicles for less money than what their used vehicle departments have to pay to acquire them.

Through my work with dealers like the Freeds at Town Motors, I have a reasonable answer. These dealers are consistently hitting home runs. The difference, however, is that their home run deals do not flow from achieving a maximum gross profit from their selling price. Instead, these dealers re-define what makes a home run deal and adjust their operations to ensure that they are able to consistently score on every deal they make.

It's worth noting that, in many ways, one-price dealers like the Freeds and CarMax are applying the same strategy that has made the retailing giant Wal-Mart highly successful. Wal-Mart's business runs on razor-thin margins. The company understands that high gross profits are unattainable. So what do they do? They embrace the low margin and aim for bigger volumes. Put another way, they make less on everything they sell, but they end up making more money because they sell a lot of everything they stock.

That is pretty much the same underlying strategy that the Freeds and retailers like CarMax use when they offer a one-price selling environment. They have recast the home run deal that has long been a staple for traditional used vehicle departments. This new type of home run deal has four key components:

1. **Inventory velocity is a religion.** The impressive, 17x turn rate that the Freeds achieve is velocity in action. They are able to achieve this by acquiring vehicles on the money and pricing them to be competitive. As a result, they have more opportunities to sell because their pricing brings them to their door more consistently than they would with a less-astute pricing strategy. With more sales opportunities, the Freeds are able to sell more vehicles. To paraphrase the movie Field of Dreams and apply it to our business, "if you price it right, they will come."

2. **They make more money.** The money-making at one-price stores flows directly from their laser-like focus on velocity. Because these dealers understand the all-important concept of purchasing vehicles to margin and pricing vehicles to market, they effectively create inventories that are bought on the money and are often more fresh than inventories at competing stores. The efficiencies they create by deploying an investment-minded

strategy that links acquisition costs, pricing and gross profit returns enable them to generate transaction profits that are consistently better their traditional dealer competitors.

If you look at these dealers' financials, you'll see they have eliminated the profit peaks and valleys that less-efficient dealers wrestle with. It's not uncommon for inefficient dealers to see an occasional deal with a $3,000 or $4,000 gross profit—alongside a string of deals that only generate $1,000 or less in gross profit and other deals that are straight-up wholesale losers.

By contrast, one-price dealers use purchasing to margin and pricing to market to determine the maximum gross profit return that every vehicle will deliver, and they hit that mark every time. It's not uncommon to see consistent gross profit averages of $2,000 at one-price stores. The dynamic here is the same thing that is occurring at Wal-Mart: lower margins and a greater volume of sales generate the overall financial success and profitability for the business.

3. **They enjoy richer F&I profits.** One-price dealers apply the same pricing strategy in F&I as they do in their sales departments. They don't negotiate on interest rate spreads or the asking price for a

service contract. They offer a single price and then help customers understand why a product and price creates added value for them. Judging from the F&I revenues I've seen at one-price stores, there's no question that this selling environment makes customers more comfortable and more receptive to purchasing products in F&I than in many traditional stores.

4. They have less variable expenses in every deal. Mark Rikess, the one-price guru from The Rikess Group who effectively introduced this retailing concept to our industry, notes that the manager to salesperson ratio at most traditional dealerships runs roughly 1:2.5. Meanwhile, the ratio typically runs about 1:4 at one-price stores. What does that mean in terms of cost on a per-deal basis? "It's not uncommon for us to see one-price dealers cut $300 or more in personnel expense, on a per-deal basis, to less than $200," Rikess says.

Such gains do stand to reason: if you take negotiation out of the sales process, you don't need as many managers overseeing the haggling between salespeople and customers. In this environment, the price is already established. Salespeople work on building trust and rapport with customers, and selling the benefits and features of a vehicle. "People with excellent negotiation skills are expensive and they're hard to retain," Rikess says. "One-price stores don't have to worry about either one of those challenges."

THE MAGIC DUST IN THE ONE-PRICE ENVIRONMENT

A lot of dealers dismiss the idea of one-price retailing out of hand by their belief that their customers like to negotiate. For them, a discussion of one-price retailing is as relevant as wondering whether the moon is made of cheese.

"People with excellent negotiation skills are expensive and they're hard to retain," Rikess says. "One-price stores don't have to worry about either one of those challenges."

I used to think this way too, until I started looking into the reasons why one-price stores were consistently building sales volumes and profits in their used vehicle departments while more traditional dealers continued to struggle.

To be sure, pricing and operational efficiencies have a huge impact on the financial statements at one-price stores. But the more I looked behind these numbers, the more I began to re-think my belief that negotiation's an essential and critical part of how you should sell a vehicle.

I went back to guys like the Freeds and Rikess to get some schooling. From what I've learned, you can't separate the culture from the financial performance of these stores. The two are inextricably tied together. One does not work without the other, and vice versa.

In addition, the culture is more than just a negotiation-free sales process. It's a way of life for these dealers and their employees. I asked a manager at a one-price store about this and his reply came out so quickly and dismissively that I still remember it today: "Nobody loses here. Customers get what they want, and we do too."

Rikess has his own read on why the culture of one-price stores resonates with today's customers. As he explains it, the reality of the Internet means many of today's customers come armed with price information for a specific vehicle when they visit a dealership. To them, the art of negotiation, while it may have appeal, is mostly an exercise with no real purpose. They know what a vehicle's worth and the negotiation process has just become a painful exercise they must endure to get to the price they know is fair and reasonable for the vehicle.

Rikess also believes that our time-pressed society contributes to this way of thinking. A negotiated sales process takes time. And, when customers realize that they're spending 45 minutes or longer to make a $5 to $25 difference in their monthly payment on a deal, it starts to feel like a waste of time. "We all trade time for money every day. Customers today don't spend an extra hour looking for any product to save $10," Rikess says.

There's no question that it's this kind of thinking that fuels the marketing messages from one-price dealers and retailers like CarMax. They flat out say: we've got a better way. And they deliver the better way with decent, knowledgeable salespeople whom customers can trust. They provide an atmosphere that, combined with a fair price on the vehicle, gives customers a more satisfying, mind-easing experience than they get in most dealerships' used vehicle departments.

I have to agree with Rikess when he says that one-price stores "typically make better net profits because they operate more efficiently, pay less employee costs and deliver a good customer experience."

Why trust is easier to achieve in one-price environments

I took up the idea of a better way with Rikess and other one-price experts. Beyond the elimination of negotiation from the sales process, what is it about the one-price environment that makes it a better way?

"It's easier for one-price stores to develop trust with customers," Rikess says.

His explanation goes something like this: just as today's customers want to trust the used vehicles they purchase, they also want to trust the people they buy from. Every sales process has a stage in which "establishing rapport/trust" is a key prong. Yet, many customers, particularly when it comes to used vehicles, don't trust the salesperson who's handling their deal. In fact, even if the salesperson is the most decent, considerate and professional person, the lack of trust is still a problem in many stores.

Why? Because the entire sales process is built around the inefficient management strategies that many franchised dealers and used vehicle managers rely upon today to run their used vehicle departments. The only thing that matters in this environment is big-grossing, home run deals and everyone works their hardest to get them.

This mentality has a corrosive effect on the sales process and the trust a salesperson is trying to create with a customer. No matter what, the salesperson *must* aim for the home run and start negotiations at an inflated price, because that's what he or she is expected to do. It's also true that our pay plans engender this behavior because they typically reward home runs more richly than they reward a consistent series of singles and doubles.

By contrast, the salespeople in one-price environments cannot shoot for traditional-style home run deals. It's not a matter of them earning salary versus commission. The reality is this: those traditional, big-dollar home run deals simply don't exist in a one-price retailing environment.

In fact, if a traditional home-run deal that grossed $4,000 showed up in a CarMax store, managers wouldn't be high-fiving each other. Instead, they'd be tearing the deal apart to find out what went wrong. Was a salesperson too pushy or dishonest? Was the vehicle priced incorrectly? Did someone make a mistake?

That type of management is 180 degrees different than what occurs at most traditional franchised dealerships. At traditional dealerships, dealers and used vehicle managers are still aiming for big gross profits and congratulating themselves when they get them. This is because they still have to make up for a variety of inefficiencies and bad decisions that occur in virtually every used vehicle's life cycle, from a too-high acquisition price, inattention to pricing and the ever-present press of an aging problem.

The whole one-price operation—from acquisition to retailing of used vehicles—is set up to make money based on turning as many vehicles at reasonable profits in the least amount of time. One price stores are far more efficient at moving iron and making money while they do it. It's velocity in action.

Now, while I may be a cheerleader for one-price retailing, I am not advocating that every franchised dealer and used vehicle manager go down the path of one-price selling. But I am saying that there are some key lessons for every franchised dealer or used vehicle manager.

First and foremost, these one-price dealers are fast becoming masters of applying investment-based thinking to the management of their used vehicle operations.

They understand that the equity of their investment in used vehicles matters and they're aggressively managing the processes they use to purchase, price and dispose of vehicles with return on investment goals in mind. They are taking advantage of purchasing and pricing inefficiencies that are making less financially sophisticated dealers and used vehicle managers struggle in their markets.

You can see why I've become a strong believer in the one-price selling model—and why the processes and approaches that dealers like the Freeds and retailers like CarMax are worth mentioning.

When you go behind the scenes, these dealers are the living embodiment of what can happen when you deploy an investment-based approach to managing your used vehicle operations. Your acquisition of vehicles gets smarter. Your pricing is more competitive. Your sales and turn rates improve. You and your managers and salespeople make more money. You have an increasing pool of satisfied customers.

I recognize that many dealers won't have the interest or stomach to investigate whether one-price selling is right for them. Nor do I think that it's necessary for every dealer. Traditional dealers who heed the idea of velocity and other investment-minded principles outlined in this book, almost by default, will be offering their customers an experience that's more transparent and straightforward than the age-old approaches to retailing used vehicles that we've all practiced for years.

Dealers and used vehicle managers who become more astute about managing the investment health of their inventories, from the moment they buy a vehicle through the stages of reconditioning, pricing and desking, will be better able to draw more leads from today's price conscious buyers and close more deals. In addition, the astute financial management will help eliminate wholesale losses and ensure more consistent, though not mind-blowing, gross profits on every unit sold.

No Pain, No Gain

Before wrapping up this book, I'd like to congratulate every reader who's stuck with me through these pages. As a second-generation dealer, I understand the difficulties and pressures of running a store, and I know full well how challenging it can be to take anything an outsider says about running a business seriously.

It can be tough to hear someone say your used vehicle pricing strategy is nothing more than a $4,000 Fantasy or that your best efforts to manage the age of your inventory effectively only amount to a no-win shell game.

But if you've come this far, you deserve a lot of credit. I've purposely pulled no punches in this book because I truly believe that franchised dealers need to wake up and embrace the new realities of today's more challenging used vehicle marketplace. I also believe, with unequivocal fervor, that the investment-minded approach to managing used vehicles that I've outlined in this book is the best recipe for success for any dealer who wants to build a profit-generating used vehicle department.

My confidence comes from the track record of successes I've seen at stores where dealers embrace these investment-minded principles and stick to their guns despite resistance from managers and salespeople.

I'll humbly state, here and now, that your own decision to adopt an investment-minded approach to used vehicle management will not come without some significant pain. You'll have to break bad habits and assumptions about this business that we've all followed and held for years. Some of you may even need to let go of trusted managers and salespeople who will resist your efforts to deploy investment-minded management principles and, in turn, hold everyone more accountable to the financial metrics that will drive profits and success in your used vehicle departments.

I hope that this book will serve as a roadmap to help you recognize and address the shortcomings that are undercutting your ability to increase sales volumes and build a greater degree of real, not imagined, profitability in your used vehicle departments.

As I've outlined in the book, an investment-minded approach to managing used vehicles affects every facet of the business—from acquisition and pricing, to desking and disposition. I've tried to show you enough real-life examples for each operational element to help you begin to change the essential elements of your used vehicle operations and begin realizing the successes that other dealers have already achieved.

While your transition to an investment-minded approach to used vehicle management will not be easy, the rewards are significant. There's an old axiom, "no pain, no gain." This statement could not be more true as you begin to migrate to a more financially sound strategy and approach to your used vehicle operations.

Like any good investment, the time and energy you put into this investment-focused mindset will bring its own rewards. And for many of you, those rewards will come at the expense of other dealers who won't know what hit them.

ABOUT THE AUTHOR

In some ways, Dale Pollak is like any other car dealer—ambitious, entrepreneurial, a student of the car business. But in other ways, Dale is different. After working as a dealer principal at a Chicago-area Cadillac store for thirteen years, Dale decided to apply his, "Could there be a better way to do this?" thinking toward helping dealers improve their operations and profitability. He was a founding member of Digital Motorworks, Inc. and subsequently launched vAuto, Inc., a software company that offers dealers a new and better way to manage their used vehicle operations.

Dale is a sought-after speaker for dealer 20 groups, association meetings and industry conferences where he shares his innovative ideas for making dealerships more efficient, effective and profitable. As a thought leader with more than 20 years as both a dealer and CEO in automotive retailing,

Dale has written for *Ward's Dealer Business, Dealer* magazine and other publications.

Dale received his B.S. in Business Administration from Indiana University and is a graduate of the General Motors Institute of Automotive Development. He also earned a law degree from DePaul University's College of Law, and is a four-time winner of the American Jurisprudence Award for top performance in his class. Dale lives in Burr Ridge, Illinois with his wife and three children.

INDEX

CPSIA information can be obtained at www.ICGtesting.com
Printed in the USA
BVOW020202230911

271930BV00002B/13/P